ANIMAL FOLKLORE,
MYTH AND LEGEND

ANIMAL FOLKLORE,
MYTH AND LEGEND

Anthony Wootton

with drawings by the author

BLANDFORD PRESS
POOLE · NEW YORK · SYDNEY

First published in the UK 1986 by Blandford Press
Link House, West Street, Poole, Dorset, BH15 1LL

Copyright © 1986 Anthony Wootton

Distributed in the United States by
Sterling Publishing Co., Inc.,
2 Park Avenue, New York, NY 10016

Distributed in Australia by
Capricorn Link (Australia) Pty Ltd
PO Box 665, Lane Cove, NSW 2066

British Library Cataloguing in Publication Data

Wootton, Anthony, *1935-*
  Animal folklore, myth and legend.
  1. Animals, Mythical
  I. Title
  398'.469   GR825

ISBN 0 7137 1617 7

Typeset by Lovell Baines Ltd, Hollington Farm, Woolton Hill, Newbury, Berkshire.

Printed in Great Britain by Biddles Ltd, Guildford

CONTENTS

Preface

1 Animals in the Language   9

2 Misconceptions and Half-truths   34

3 Anthropomorphism – Or Is It?   52

4 Animal Weather Signs and Other Sensitives   62

5 Fears and Phobias   70

6 Dangers, Real and Imagined   88

7 An Animal *Materia Medica*   99

8 Legends, Ancient and Modern   115

9 Myth to Reality?   126

10 The Search for Living Monsters   142

Bibliography   156

Index   159

PREFACE

'Man ... is a being born to believe.' – Benjamin Disraeli (1804–81).

As children, most of us are nurtured on tales about animals – tales that frequently bear little, if any, relation to accepted zoological fact. Stories of man-eating giants, dragons and other fabulous beasts, of 'real' animals anthropomorphised into speaking, dressing and behaving like people, are often the lineal descendants of far more ancient myths and legends which, in former times, attracted a far wider audience, of all ages and classes, who often believed in them implicitly.

Today's vastly increased knowledge of animals and their ways may incline many of us to scorn or smile at these fables when we come to man's estate, yet the fact is that they exert a greater influence on our lives than is often realised. Many of the deep-rooted misconceptions about and prejudices towards animals, notably with reference to their supposed dangerousness, owe their persistence to the fact that we gained our attitudes to them from such stories, perhaps via our parents, who were doubtless similarly 'indoctrinated' by theirs, and so back into the mists of time. Half-truths and hidden meanings probably lie at the root of a host of other ancient animal legends and traditional beliefs, as well as many of those hybrid beasts of the world's mythologies; while a plethora of animal references, often obscure and inaccurate but always fascinating to unravel, have found their way into our everyday language, most of them used without our being aware that we are referring to animals at all! Nor is our latterday credulity of an entirely passive nature: witness the deep interest still taken by many people, both scientists and laymen, in the possibility of apemen or huge dinosaur-like beasts still existing in remote areas.

Such things form the subject of this book which, at the risk of appearing pretentious, I would describe as one for the naturalist who is interested in folklore, rather than the other way about, since one of my primary concerns has been to explore those topics which I felt might be susceptible of some sort of logical, zoological explanation.

I have used the terms 'Folklore', 'myth' and 'legend' in the book's title quite deliberately since, while the three tend to shade into each other to a certain degree, there is, nevertheless, a subtle difference between them. Apart from its basic meaning of falsehood, a *myth* I take to be more of a concept, commonly but not invariably involving purely fictional animals. A *legend* is, in general, a story or narrative, linked for the most part to existing animals, however fancified. *Folklore* – literally 'folk knowledge' – is essentially traditional, grass-roots wisdom, typically handed down by word of mouth and applied in particular to such topics as observing animals' links with weather changes or their use in primitive medicine.

Even within the book's limitations, a considerable body of literature was consulted during its compilation, and the more important of these books are listed in the bibliography: to have included articles and papers would have rendered it altogether unwieldy. I am also indebted to a whole host of friends, correspondents and institutions who provided me with information or assistance or who were able to clarify various points, among them: The Bodleian Library, Oxford; Buckinghamshire County Library, Aylesbury; Dr Maurice Burton; the BBC Natural History Unit, Bristol; Mr L.R.H. Smith, Keeper of Oriental Antiquities, The British Museum; The Director, Musei Capitolini, Rome; Mrs Elli Dunkin; Dr N. Humburg, Curator, Hameln Museum; The Rev. A.D. Jones; The Librarian, Pharmaceutical Society of Great Britain; Mrs D. Kirby, Principal Pharmacist, Stoke Mandeville Hospital, Aylesbury; The Curator, Pitt Rivers Museum, Oxford; and the editors of a number of magazines, including *BBC Wildlife, Shooting Times & Country Magazine*, and *Country Quest*, for publishing my letters appealing for information. Other sources are acknowledged in the text.

A.W. 1986

1·ANIMALS IN THE LANGUAGE

LIKE ANIMALS

English-speaking peoples are notoriously careless and inaccurate in their use of the language, and never more so than when referring to animals. Even the word animal itself comes in for such mistreatment. Zoologically and, indeed, in every other context it ought to refer, and actually does, to any living organism that is not a plant; but that is not the way it is used in common parlance. To most people, 'animal' is basically a synonym for 'mammal', which is why we find semi-tautologies like 'animals and birds' or 'animals and insects' littering the English tongue, the implication being that neither birds nor, more especially, insects are 'proper' animals at all.

Given this, it is not difficult to appreciate why, when people call themselves or their children animal-lovers, they are being rather less all-inclusive than the expression suggests to the literally-minded zoologist. What they really mean, of course, is that they prefer the company of and have a greater empathy with warm-blooded animals that display certain vaguely human features (like large, appealing eyes) and may also respond rather more positively to their attentions. That people's anthropomorphic 'love' rarely extends to snakes and beetles, spiders or worms is perhaps understandable, but we really should say what we mean.

In view of the affection that inhabitants of the western world, in particular, commonly profess for their fellow creatures, it has always struck me as curious that the word animal can also be used in an equally inaccurate and far more aspersive sense. To suggest that someone or some group has behaved *like* an animal (or wild beast) is to accuse them of plumbing the very depths of moral degradation: no description could be more damning. Basic contradiction apart, it is difficult to appreciate why this should be so, since no animal murders, rapes, vandalises, or is guilty of any of the other innumerable failings that man's flesh is heir to: these are purely human concepts which we transfer, quite erroneously and unjustifiably, to animals, rather as if we were desperately trying to find someone or something to share or shoulder the (our) blame.

9

Animals may be *a*moral, and 'know no better', but they are certainly not *im*moral. Indeed, the sobering fact is that, despite lacking our moral codes, they rarely stray far from a pattern of behaviour that inflicts the very minimum of suffering or inconvenience on other species. When an animal attacks or kills another, it is almost invariably either for food or in defence of its territory or young: there are no hidden motives of jealousy or greed. An animal that abandons or even eats its own offspring is not being unnecessarily cruel, merely reacting to a situation that makes it better for the more valuable parent to sacrifice them and start again and, at the same time, perhaps, not waste their substance. A female mantis or spider cannibalising her mate is similarly acting out of purely practical, unemotional considerations: the male will soon die anyway and his body proteins help his partner to survive the energy-consuming business of egg-maturation and care of the young. It is perhaps worth reminding ourselves that cannibalism or consumption of the recent departed is, and certainly was, not unknown in human societies.

Nature's tooth may indeed be red and raw, but only because death in the animal world is simple, open and direct. Our own killing for food is infinitely more brutal and generally glossed over and hidden from those who eat meat but prefer not to think overmuch about its production and supply; and that is to say nothing of the many other cruelties we inflict on animals for far less justifiable reasons or the readiness with which we 'put down' ailing or simply old pets in a way which would be totally unacceptable where humans were concerned. The strange thing is that whereas animals may be assumed to have no conscience, and no need of one, since they are without sin, our own possession of this occasionally inhibiting moral sense does not save us from continuing to hurt both our fellow man and other creatures, even when we know what we do is wrong.

As we shall see, a great many of the adjectives we apply to animals and their behaviour are not merely grossly unfair and aspersive but betray ignorance of their basic meaning. When animals are described as 'vicious' – generally they are the ones that fight back when threatened or hurt – they are actually being accused of peculiarly human failings, or vices. Nor are animals 'bloodthirsty', an expression that implies killing for its own sake. One or two animals (stoats, for example) do sip the blood of their victims, but the only inveterate blood-drinkers of the animal world are the vampire bats and insects like mosquitoes, fleas and lice; and all of these animals' bloodthirstiness is no more than an individualistic way of obtaining sustenance.

Anyone thinking to discern evidence of other vices or sins like envy, pride or avarice will find, on closer investigation, that they are geared solely to survival or the perpetuation of their kind. An animal may occasionally over-eat and appear 'gluttonous', like the European glutton or wolverine, but its apparent greed makes good sense, since it is quite possible it may not have another chance of a meal for some considerable time. It could even, subsequent to its meal, appear 'slothful' (see page 12), except that proper digestion necessitates such a period of inactivity, as it does with us. Lust is similarly foreign to animals' nature. When animals do mate indiscriminately and even, as in ducks, appear to force their attentions on unwilling females, the answer lies solely in the drakes' enthusiasm to spread and perpetuate their genes. Nor is that merely playing with words since, unlike truly lustful man, birds and other animals generally only come into breeding condition for short periods each year and need to mate while they can. Presumably, there is some 'animal' pleasure in the business, too, but we can be pretty sure it is merely incidental and hardly even a secondary consideration!

SIMILES AND METAPHORS

Whether real or imagined, animals' physical and behavioural attributes have enriched the English language with a wealth of allusiveness in simile and metaphor. Strength and weakness, industry and guile, wisdom and stupidity, these and more are all idealised in our fellow creatures, from the highest to the low. A man might be 'as brave as a lion' or 'as strong as a bear', both creatures finding their way into heraldry in implying that the princely bearers of such symbols shared these highly desirable qualities. A bear could be, in turn, both lovable and bad-tempered. To suggest that someone is 'a bit of a bear' implies that he might be strong, and even rather over*bear*ing, but is really quite gentle with it, even when giving a friend a 'bear hug' (which no bear does, incidentally). To be a 'bear with a sore head' implies irritability, apparently based on the presumed tetchiness of a hungry bear just emerged from its winter hibernation. The head of a bear was long thought to be its weakest point and that it was even possible for a brave man to kill one with a single blow of his fist. No wonder a bear was bad- tempered if its head ached! At the other extreme of animal size, to be described as a mouse implies not merely diminished stature but extreme timidity and lack of spirit; a 'mousy' person combines dowdiness with colourlessness, greyish or drab like a mouse's fur. If you are a worm, you are clearly spineless and without any hint of boldness or bravery. To be 'bird-like' suggests daintiness and delicacy, applied especially to dear old ladies.

To be as 'busy as a bee' (or beaver) is an accurate enough observation and as justified as the well-known biblical exhortation to match the hard-working nature of the ant (*Proverbs* vi, 6). During one's labour one might whistle and thus be as 'cheerful as a cricket', though the borrowing here is less accurate, since a cricket's shrillings are not so much an indication of happiness as a courtship call.

Significantly, there appear to be few verbal borrowings from the animal kingdom to suggest laziness and indolence. 'Slothful', referred to earlier, may seem to be one such, but is really an example of the process in reverse, since the word sloth (Middle English *slowthe*, slow) has been with us considerably longer than our knowledge of these strange, slow-moving Central and South American edentates. More definite extremes derive from animals like the fox and ox, the one presenting the imagined acme of cunning and deviousness, presumably based on its astuteness in outwitting the hunter (with a bit of anthropomorphism linked to its facial 'mask' and sly appearance thrown in), and the other of dullness, slowness and stupidity, albeit coupled with strength. Foolish obtuseness might also be applied to the donkey, a domesticated descendant of the wild ass (*Equus asinus*) of North Africa and Asia. It is from the ass's scientific epithet that we derive the adjective asinine, though neither asses nor donkeys are at all stupid: if anything, rather the reverse. A mule, the result of pairing a female horse with a male ass, might occasionally be stubborn but probably only because, like many a hybrid, it is in reality brighter than average and has its own ideas of how and what things should be done.

Physical evidences of lunacy are implicit in the expression 'as mad as a March hare', based on the curiously erratic behaviour of the bucks or 'jacks' during early spring courtship. Bats are not blind (see page 75), but to be 'batty' or have 'bats in the belfry' also indicates things are not quite as they should be in the upper storey. The cuckoo and the coot have similarly long been used metaphorically to suggest a certain silliness or craziness, the former from its call (which also gives us *cuckold*: a husband duped like the luckless foster-parents forced to rear a young cuckoo parasite) and the latter, presumably, from its wild dashings over the water in seeing off rivals. Both coot and badger also provide similes for human baldness, based on their partially white heads.

Peculiarly human failings like grossness of appetite are catered for in references to the feeding habits of pigs (or hogs) and that weasel-relative, the glutton. If you were really far gone on ale or mead or, worse, opium, you were figuratively as 'high' as the kites which used to scavenge over mediaeval London and soar and hover (like the toy) at a considerable height. A 'kite' was also a rapacious person, and the raven was regarded in a similar light. Nowadays, to be ravenous is merely to be exceedingly hungry, but its original meaning probably included overtones of cruelty or death-dealing, since this largest member of the crow family is not averse to attacking sickly lambs in addition to scavenging on dead ones.

The *Corvidae* have a justifiable reputation for acquisitiveness and this,

12

too, has produced some interesting extensions to the human condition. To 'rook' someone is to steal or pull a fast one on them, in clear reference to the way rooks occasionally thieve twigs from the nests of their neighbours. Anyone with a 'magpie instinct' likes collecting all manner of trinkets and gew-gaws, just as magpies (and jackdaws) are strangely and inexplicably attracted to glittering items, which they commonly store in their nests. If, on the other hand, you are merely *in*quisitive, you might be described as an earwig or as 'earwigging', particularly if you listen to conversations that are none of your business. The word might also be used in the sense of gossiping: you 'gained the ear' of someone, just as these much maligned insects have long been supposed to do. (page 23).

Since we accuse animals of just about every sin under the sun, tacitly or otherwise, it is scarcely surprising to find that some of the less popular ones are the particular targets of our opprobrium, with linguistic expressions to match. Of these, rats and snakes provide ideal subjects, at least in the popular estimation. To 'rat' on someone is to renege on an agreement or betray a friend and, since the rodents still tend to be thought of as uncleanly, in Cagney's 'You dirty rat!' we seem to have it all. 'Cowardly' in leaving a sinking ship, 'vicious' when cornered, rats have also provided an ill-founded metaphor for bad-temperedness: 'ratty'. A 'snake in the grass' is an equally low, treacherous creature, as is the 'viper in my bosom', nurtured by a sorrowing mother.

Sexism, too, has found its way from the animal world into the English language. To be 'as strong as a bull', even if one were 'bull-headed', might be acceptable enough, but to describe a woman as a cow was, and is, scarcely complimentary. The same applies to 'bitch', or the somewhat outmoded but equally derogatory and wholly female 'shrew'. Linked to the long-standing belief that these fierce, little, long-snouted insectivores had a venomous bite, a human shrew was an inquisitive, venomous-tongued, nagging woman, and quite probably a witch to boot. 'Shrewd', deriving from the same source, has a more general application. Nowadays it means astute and calculating but originally suggested knavishness and rascality, characters which know no sexual bounds.

FIGURES OF SPEECH

Nowadays, when someone or something is 'licked into shape', he or it is merely polished up or rendered efficient from ungainly or untidy beginnings, but the expression ultimately derives from the old belief that a she-bear had, quite literally, to lick her misshapen newborn cubs into bear form. The idea, which seems to have been widely and genuinely believed until about the seventeenth century, goes back at least to classical times and is borrowed by Shakespeare in his *Henry VI*, Part 3, wherein the hunchbacked Duke of Gloucester (the future Richard III) likens himself, rather self-pityingly, to 'an unlick'd bear-whelp that carries no impression like the dam'.

Goats were long regarded as the epitome of lecherousness and associated with the cloven-hooved Pan, the Roman god of nature, and, through his witches, who rode on the backs of goats, the devil himself. Thus, anyone who behaved in a goatish manner, or 'acted the goat', was both dissipated and immoral. Later, the goat reference became somewhat softened to suggest someone who, like a 'giddy goat' butting at anything and anybody, merely played the fool. Goats have found their way into the language in other senses, too. To 'separate the sheep from the goats' implies sorting the docile and manageable elements from the more erratic, wilder ones. Its precise origins seem obscure and may be at least partly zoological since, anatomically at least, sheep and goats are difficult to distinguish and may be impossible to classify one way or the other from bones excavated at archaeological sites. Sheep were not originally domesticated for their wool, but for their meat, and since the two are otherwise very similar physically it must often have been quite difficult to distinguish sheep from goats if the two were kept in the same area, despite their display of certain differences in temperament and feeding. Present-day goats are liable to nibble at anything vegetable and are almost as agile in reaching it on rocky precipices as their wild ancestors, whereas sheep are better adapted for low-level grazing. With this in mind, there are still hill farmers today who keep goats with their sheep so that they may browse the upper areas and prevent their less sure-footed relatives from putting themselves at risk by climbing higher in search of food.

'Scapegoat' is another interesting caprine expression of considerable antiquity. Nowadays we use the term for an individual who is forced to shoulder the blame for some act of collective wrong-doing. The original scape-goat was a 'real' goat which, in *Leviticus* xvi, 7–10, God orders to be allocated to him as bearing the combined sins of the people. The animal was thus symbolically made the (e)scape-goat for man.

Pigs find their way into such expressions as 'a pig in a poke', which implies a somewhat doubtful purchase. The phrase is said to derive from Anglo-Saxon times when suckling pigs were habitually taken to market in a sack, or poke. Unfortunately, there were frequently shady characters who substituted a rather less valuable animal, such as a cat, for the piglet, thus making it advisable to examine one's purchases closely before parting with cash. A slightly different kind of risky undertaking is inherent in 'white elephant', which currently means any purchase or gift whose maintenance proves more trouble than it is worth. The original white elephant appears to derive from Siam (now Thailand), whose king might give a neighbouring ruler a white elephant, knowing full well that its upkeep would involve the recipient in considerable expense, and that he would not be able to get rid of it without causing grave offence.

Some mammalian expressions appear to have their origins in the New World, although their present-day use is widespread throughout English-speaking countries. 'Playing possum' means lying low or even shamming death, and clearly derives from the American opossum's habit of falling into a sort of cataleptic trance when seized by a predator, even to the extent of allowing itself to be violently shaken and chewed. If you are 'barking up the wrong tree' you are completely on the wrong track during some investigation, line of thought or argument. Dogs, it seems, would occasionally quite literally bark up the wrong tree during the hunting of raccoons, which commonly sought sanctuary in its branches.

More than one bird expression has its origins in the USA, too. The first 'stool-pigeons' seem to have been employed by hunters who tied a pigeon to a stool as a movable lure for attracting its fellows within range; later, its meaning shifted to describe a police suspect who, whilst being 'tied down' and interrogated, might also hopefully inform on his accomplices and become a 'stoolie'. Domestic fowl provide a number of picturesque allusions, among them 'cock-sure' or 'cocky': showily self-confident like the proud farmyard rooster crowing over his harem of hens; 'cock-a-hoop' was perhaps rather noisily triumphant, like the cockerel with his scarlet *hoop*, or crest, erect. An entertainer 'given the bird' might be hissed after the manner of a goose, and a politician harangued or 'heckled', the latter perhaps originally referring either to the derisive-sounding call of the heckle (originally 'hack-wall'), or green woodpecker, or to the raised *hackles* (short feathers) on a cockerel's neck.

Until one probes deeper, some avian expressions seem quite absurd and inconsequential. If a gamekeeper or other person is described as being able to 'tell a hawk from a handsaw', he clearly knows his business, although the expression owes nothing to carpentry or tree-felling. *Handsaw* or *hanser* is an Old English name for the heron (*Ardea cinerea*), so that our original countryman was, like Hamlet (Act II, Scene 2), merely a moderately good ornithologist. 'Swan-song', the farewell performance of, say, a composer or musician, sounds equally unlikely, since swans are not particularly vocal and certainly have no song, as such; yet the ancient belief that a swan sings sweetly just before it dies (presumably at the prospect of a happier existence to come), and at no other time in its life, may not be entirely unfounded if reports from American wildfowlers are to be relied upon.

No-one would be likely to shoot a swan in Britain today, since the birds are protected by law. If he did so accidentally he might be regretful and even shed tears of regret, but they would not, one hopes, be like those of the crocodile, which according to the well-known linguistic borrowing weeps in patently false contrition. The direct observation is accurate enough in itself, since 'tears' (more precisely, lachrymal fluid) *are* commonly exuded when a crocodile or alligator seizes and mangles its prey, and flow with particular copiousness during times of stress or emotion, as in feeding. Their main purpose, however, is to keep the eye moist and clean and there is, needless to say, no hint of sorrow in the crocodile's weeping.

The crocodile's apparent hypocrisy is further emphasised by what appears to be its permanent, open-mouthed grin, as it waits for suitable victims to approach: a point remarked upon by Alice (in Wonderland) with particular reference to fish, which also provide us with another widely-used expression. Should we find ourselves with 'a pretty kettle of fish', we are more likely to have a problem than a good potential meal, although the latter would seem to be nearer its original meaning. Apparently, it was once the custom in the border regions of Scotland and England to enjoy alfresco meals of salmon on the riverside, where the fish were caught and cooked in a *kettle* or cooking pan. The fish were 'pretty' in the sense of tricky (Old English *praettig*), since catching and landing salmon demanded (and demands) a degree of skill and patience.

Bites of a kind quite different from those obtained by angling might be gained at a 'flea-market', which must originally have been just the sort of place where it would have been easy to pick up fleas and lice from unwashed patrons. It is said that the original flea-market is the famous *Marche aux Puces* (Market of Fleas) in Paris, which sells secondhand clothes, particularly suitable for harbouring these annoying parasites. Fleas have also found their way into the language in the sense of sending a person away 'with a flea in his ear': in other words, with a stinging rebuke or correction, analogous to the bite of a flea. 'Lousy', it is interesting to note, nowadays seems to have departed completely from its original insect connection and assumed the colloquial sense of useless or poor quality.

MISLEADING EPITHETS

A great many of the titles and descriptive names we afford animals present a misleading impression of their nature and relationships. Some are understandable enough, like the so-called Barbary 'apes' (*Macaca sylvanus*) which live not only on the famous Rock but across the narrow Straits of Gibraltar in Morocco and Algeria. Apes are indeed invariably tail-less, but the animals in question are really rather unusual monkeys, related to the macaques, some of which have long tails, short stumps or, like *Macaca sylvanus*, none at all. The Australian koala (*Phascolarctus cinerus*), typically 'teddy-like' through it appears, is not at all related to the bears but is a marsupial, bearing its young in a pouch, like the kangaroos, wallabies, wombats and opossums. In Britain, the name water-rat is commonly applied to the water-vole (*Arvicola amphibius*), which typically dives into the water at any human approach along the river bank. True rats (*Rattus*) can swim well, too, but differ from the vole in being generally rather bigger, with sharper face, more prominent ears and much longer, almost hairless tail, the water-vole's tail being hairier.

Confusion often arises from the application of quite different popular names to particular animals in widely separated English-speaking countries. Thus, 'buffalo', long applied to the North American bison, should really refer to superficially similar oxen of Africa and Asia, commonly used for traction and ploughing. What British naturalists know as the bottle-nosed dolphin (*Tursiops truncatus*) the Americans commonly call a porpoise, although true porpoises, which lack the dolphin's snout, belong to a separate family (Phocoenidae) from the dolphins (Delphinidae). Another true dolphin is the so-called killer whale (*Orcinus orca*). Similar transatlantic nomenclatorial differences also apply to what the British and Americans consider to be turtles and tortoises. In the United States, 'turtle' tends to be applied to the whole of the Testudines, terrestrial tortoises, including those commonly kept as pets, being referred to as land turtles. It is perhaps worth adding that 'the voice of the turtle' mentioned in the biblical *Song of Solomon* actually refers to the turtle dove. None of the turtle/tortoise tribe has much of a voice, the most they can do being to hiss and roar by expelling air through their nostrils, more particularly when irritated or during courtship and mating.

Among birds, the barnacle goose (*Branta leucopsis*), principally an arctic species which winters on the shores of northern Europe, is of particular nominal interest, since the origin of its name lies not, as might be supposed, in any liking the geese might have for barnacles but in a mediaeval legend that told of the birds actually developing from the similarly pied goose barnacles (*Lepas anatifera*), which display a certain fanciful resemblance to the bird when opened out. So great was the eye of faith, it seems, that an archdeacon in the reign of England's Henry II recorded actually seeing 'more than a thousand of these birds hanging from one piece of timber on the shore enclosed in their shells and already formed'!

Barnacles, incidentally, are crustaceans and not molluscs or 'shellfish', although the epithet 'fish' has long been applied indiscriminately and inaccurately to a whole range of marine animals. Jelly-fish (Coelenterata), star-fish (Asteroidea), cuttle-fish (Decapoda) are just a few, all of them

17

belonging to separate invertebrate classes of animals quite unrelated to the backboned fishes. In fishmongerese, 'shell-fish' might include not merely molluscs like oysters, cockles, mussels and whelks but even lobsters and crabs. Should such traders offer horseshoe 'crabs' they would be equally incorrect, since these curious living fossils are really relatives of the spiders and scorpions. 'Rock salmon', on the other hand, would seem to be a rather more deliberately deceptive term, the fish in question being really dogfish, usually *Scyliorhinus canicula*, the lesser spotted dogfish.

Nominal misapplication is especially typical of the insects and invertebrates, presumably because of the indifference or even downright opprobrium with which they have long been regarded. 'Insect' itself tends to be applied indiscriminately to almost any small creeping animal with a great many legs, from spiders to centipedes, but should of course only be applied to the Hexapoda (literally 'six-legged'), an alternative scientific name for the class. 'Bug' has similarly specific entomological reference, being restricted to two particular orders (some say sub-orders) of insects, principally characterised by their retractable, tube-like piercing mouthparts; yet in popular parlance the term is used for almost anything of an obnoxious nature, including bacteria and viruses! The popular names of some individual groups of true bugs present an equally misleading idea of their nature and relationships. Water-scorpions, for example, have no kinship with scorpions and are quite harmless, and are

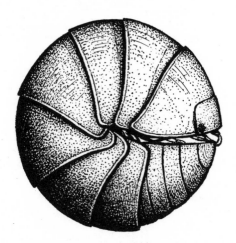

Armadillium woodlouse. Woodlice are not insects, as their 'lice' epithet suggests, but terrestrial crustaceans, allied to the marine crabs and lobsters. Pill woodlice like this were at one time swallowed as cure-all pills or hung about the necks of teething infants. Actual size (diameter) c. 5–7 mm.

so named purely on account of the superficial resemblance of the insects' enlarged forelegs to the pincers of the stinging arachnids. Woodlice and water-fleas are similarly misnamed: both are actually crustaceans, whereas true lice and fleas are, again, insects. Called sow-bugs in America, woodlice are the only crustaceans to live on land. Water-fleas would appear to be so-called because of their erratic dancing movements in the water, mildly reminiscent of jumping fleas.

'Worm' is yet another widely misapplied epithet. Slow-worm or blind-worm (legless lizard), silk-worm (moth caterpillar), wood-worm (beetle), wire-worm (beetle larva) are just some of a whole host of small animals with no kinship to the Annelida or their relatives. 'Glow-worm' is another and of particular interest since it is attached to quite different insects at far extremes of the world: in Britain to a luminescent beetle (more especially the flightless female), and in New Zealand to the larva of a fly, *Arachnocampa luminosa*, each displaying very different habits.

Entomological ignorance has also resulted in the application of misnomers to those singing insects, the crickets, grasshoppers and cicadas, the first two belonging to the Orthoptera, and the cicadas to the Homoptera (bugs). Cicadas, especially the seventeen-year cicada (*Magicicada septemdecim*), are commonly referred to as 'locusts' in the United States, from their tendency to hatch from the subterranean nymphs almost synchronously and in very large numbers, more so in some years than others. In France, *cigale* can mean, in popular patois, either cicada or certain bush-crickets.

Epithets indicating provenance also tend to be inaccurate, more especially where the animals concerned are unpopular. The various species of household cockroach, for example, are afforded titles which imply apportioning blame for their origins in quite the wrong quarters. The common or oriental cockroach (*Blatta orientalis*), popularly but, of course, erroneously called 'black beetle', the American cockroach (*Periplaneta americana*) and the German cockroach (*Blatella germanica*) – which retaliatory Germans insist on calling French – are equally misnamed, both popularly and scientifically, since it seems probable that all three ultimately emanate from Africa or perhaps the Middle East. These adaptable, omnivorous insects, equally at home in buildings and on ships, have managed through commerce to establish themselves in almost every part of the world. It is just that no one country seems to want to own them!

COLLOQUIALISMS
Individual animals are commonly referred to by several different popular names, even in the same country and language. They may be the result of

dialectal differences or simply archaic names that have largely fallen out of fashion and perhaps lingered on in a rather different sense. Many betray interesting beliefs, allusions or folklore. *Urchin*, the Old English name for the European hedgehog (*Erinaceus europaeus*), appears to date back at least to the fourteenth century, and is nowadays more likely to be applied to grimy little boys who ferret about in muck and rubbish, not unlike their prickly counterparts. Old-time countrymen, half convinced that the urchin's constantly wet snout, ripe odour and grubbing habits indicated porcine affinities, afforded it the pig's gender names, boar and sow.

Real pigs give rise to the old country name of *crowl*, to indicate the runt, or smallest of the litter, and it is possible that people bearing that surname today had ancestors who were not of the largest, just as those with the name of *Fitch*, or variants thereof, may have emitted an odour rather the reverse of violets. *Fitcher* or *fitchet* was once a widely used term for the polecat or 'fou(1)mart' (*Putorius putorius*), which emits a vile-smelling liquid when alarmed: hence the term 'to stink like a polecat' or 'fitchet'.

Among the more interesting alternatively-named birds is the stormy petrel (*Hydrobates pelagicus*), also called Mother Carey's chicken. 'Petrel' is said to derive from St Peter because of the birds' ability to patter or 'walk' over the surface of the sea, even in stormy weather. (St Peter, it will be remembered, walked on the Sea of Galilee). Commonly seen following ships, these strictly pelagic, or sea-going, birds were considered to be the attendants of a witch, although their descriptive name is really a corruption of Mater Cara, the Beloved Mother, in other words the Virgin Mary. Their appearance was long believed to actually forecast the approach of storms.

The little European freshwater fish called bullhead (*Cottus gobio*) is so named because of its enlarged flattened head which, together with its natural camouflage, helps it to avoid detection as it lies on the beds of unpolluted rivers and streams. A much older, mediaeval name for it was miller's thumb, the allusion here being to the flattening the corn-grinder's digit received from constantly testing the quality of his meal between finger and thumb. Possibly the connection came about because mills were situated by fast-flowing waters where the fish could be found.

Reference has been made elsewhere to the misleadingly named slow-worm or blind-worm (*Anguis fragilis*), which is in fact a legless lizard. Other local names for it were glass worm and glass snake, in reference both to its highly polished skin – literally as smooth as a mirror – and to a habit it shares with many lizards of shedding part of its tail when handled. The break is absolutely clean and presumably painless, the ready fracture occurring across the body of a vertebra and not, as might be thought,

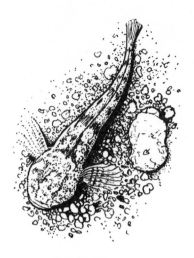

The bullhead or 'miller's thumb' (***Cottus gobio***).

between two of them. Principally a device to confuse predators, the reaction is rendered especially effective in that the shed portion often continues to wriggle for a while, thus confusing the attacker and allowing its former possessor to make good its escape. The names of some other reptiles, as well as amphibians like toads and newts, evoke interest in providing an insight into the idiosyncrasies and development of the English language. 'Adder', for example, was originally *nadder*, literally 'a creeping thing'; 'natterjack', a species of toad, derives from the same root. The first of these names comes clumsily off the tongue when prefaced with the indefinite article, which probably also explains why the original *ewt* (or *eft*) was transformed into 'newt'. Country people nowadays tend to use the older name for the land-living, or non-breeding newts, which are thus commonly called 'dry efts', not simply in reference to their terrestrial habits but because of a tendency to desiccate readily if they are prevented access to moisture.

A number of colloquial animal synonyms embellish our language in the sense of providing what would seem to be the origins of ostensibly quite unrelated expressions. A case in point is 'humbug', which in some English counties, notably Worcestershire, is applied to the large, free-flying cockchafer beetle, commonly called May 'bug' (*Melolontha melolontha*), whose powerful flight produces a loud buzzing sound. The beetle cannot sting, despite the female's impressively-pointed ovipositor, so a hum-bug (originally 'bee-beetle' or 'bee-bug', from the German and Dutch *hummel/hommel*, a bumble-bee) is a fraud or show-off, like its human counterpart. A comparable meaning is implicit in the *dor* of 'dor-beetle', an epithet applied to certain moderately large blue-black dung-beetles

21

(*Geotrupes*) that fly after dark in search of ordure in which to lay their eggs. *Dora* is Old English for bumble-bee: another obvious reference to the beetle's droning flight, which Thomas Gray makes such happy use of in his famous *Elegy*. 'Dormouse', on the other hand, has a quite different origin. Here, the 'dor' prefix is from the Old English *dorm*, which in turn probably derives from the Latin verb *dormire*, to sleep, and may also be linked to the French *dormeuse*, a sleeper, the dormouse (*Muscardinus avellanarius*) being a sound-sleeping winter hibernator.

Dragonflies are afforded a variety of evocative country names, among them 'horse-stinger', 'silver-pin' and 'devil's darning-needle', the last two applied in particular to the smaller, thin-bodied damselflies (which belong to a sub-order of the Odonata). Rather curiously, there are still today many otherwise intelligent people who are convinced that dragonflies are capable of stinging. They cannot, of course, and the rustic epithet presumably derives from the predatory dragonflies' habit of flying about horses in pursuit of attracted flies, which are captured in full flight with the aid of the sort of basket formed by their bristly, forwardly-directed legs.

The names of some insects betray a certain religious inference. Ladybirds (called lady-bugs in America, though they are really beetles) were the 'little birds' of the Virgin Mary, and therefore lucky, the seven-spot (*Coccinella septem-punctata*) especially so since it carried the mystically correct number of spots. Others are clearly onomatopoeic, among them 'katydid', an epithet for certain large bush-crickets, whose stridulatory calls sound, to some, like 'katy-did' oft repeated.

Moths bear a whole galaxy of popular names indicative of folklore and allusiveness of various kinds. The day-flying Mother Shipton (*Euclidemera mi*) gains its title, it seems, from the witch-like profile clearly discernible on its forewings, the original lady being a sixteenth-century semi-mythical witch-seer. The vapourer moth (*Orgyia antiqua*) was so titled in the eighteenth century, when a 'vapourer' was a dandy or braggart, the reference here being presumably to the species' gaudy caterpillar, since the adult (male) moth is of undistinguished colour and pattern and the female even wingless. By contrast, the goat-moth (*Cossus cossus*) is so named, not because of its appearance but from its characteristic odour, especially noticeable in the livid yellow and blood-blister red larvae, which consume the heart-wood of various sickly trees and may even betray their presence via their unusual aroma. Its scientific name rather suggests that the goat moth's larva was the *cossus* of the Romans, esteemed by their gourmets as a culinary delicacy. It is, however, more likely that the titbits in question were the larvae of certain large longhorn beetles, which also feed on wood, especially since Pliny (*Natural History*) tells of their ability to produce a shrill sound (stridulation) and also refers to the adults' long antennae. Apparently the larvae were fattened for the table on meal, rather as edible snails (*Helix pomatia*) were and still are today.

QUESTIONABLE ORIGINS

As anyone who habitually consults dictionaries will know, by no means all words in the English language are capable of tracing to source with any certainty. Such doubt attaches to many animal names, numbers of which are only to be found in anthologies of dialectal terms, where they may or (more usually) may not be explained etymologically. 'Mollern', an epithet widely used in England, especially the Midlands, for the common heron (*Ardea cinerea*), is a particular puzzle. *Erne* is straightforward enough, meaning simply a bird or in some contexts an eagle (see page 26), but what of *moll*? One possibility is that it is a semi-affectionate shortening of Molly (a diminutive of Margaret), comparable with similar titles afforded to other birds, such as Jenny wren. Some support for the idea comes from the fact that the heron is itself called Jenny or Jemmy in parts of northern England and Scotland and is also afforded praenomens like Jack and Tammie (hern), in addition to the cognomen Frank, which is clearly an onomatopoeic rendering of the bird's single-note cry. Therein *may* lie the answer, but there are other possibilities, too, among them a fancied likeness of the heron's head, rakish head-plume and long neck to a maul hammer (Latin *malleus*) or to the action of that tool when the bird stabs down at its fishy prey. Since the 'moll' syllable is lengthened in some areas to maul-erne or mawl-hern, the notion is not without a certain plausibility.

Earwig is a name conducive of even greater speculation. Most dictionaries tell us its derivation is from the Anglo-Saxon *eare*, ear, and *wicga*, a runner or wiggler, in apparent reference to the insect's supposed propensity for the human ear. The belief is shared by many countries throughout Europe, in particular (see page 85) and is difficult to explain since on the whole it is questionable if earwigs are any more prone to ear-entering than any other insect. Indeed, if the particular suspicion with which the earwig is regarded were not so ingrained and of such allegedly ancient pedigree one would be tempted to feel that it is all a misunderstanding, since its name is susceptible of various alternative etymological explanations. Some maintain that it is really ear-*wing*, reflecting the admittedly somewhat ear-like shape of the earwig's wings when opened out, but the theory is difficult to sustain since the common earwig (*Forficula auricularia*), at least, is a reluctant flier, and colloquial names nearly always derive from some frequently observed feature. More plausibly, others suggest that the 'ear' of earwig actually refers to an undeveloped flower-head, more especially, as in today's usage, an ear of corn; and that *wig* is from the Old English (Anglo-Saxon) *wic*, meaning a hiding place or dwelling – a common suffix in English place-names. Taken together, the two words thus reflect the earwig's habit, familiar to every gardener, of concealing itself in the buds and tight foliage of plants. A correspondent of mine adds yet another possibility. He believes that *ear* arises from the same root as in wheatear, a bird with a conspicuous white (*hwit*) rump (*oers*). This, coupled with our original *wicga*, therefore gives us 'arse-waggler': certainly a neat description of the earwig's ready tendency to raise and spread its terminal pincers when threatened! The earwig's forceps prompt further nominal delvings, since the French name for the common species is *perce-oreille*, or 'ear-piercer', though not, it seems, in any horrific sense. The reference here is apparently to the special tool once used by Parisian and other jewellers for piercing the ear lobes preparatory to earring suspension. There is certainly a close resemblance between that artefact and the male earwig's pincers (see illustration, page 87), and if the folklorish link between earwigs and the ears could be proved to be a relatively recent conceit one might visualise a situation where the French name – which dates at least to 1530 – became distorted by other European countries into a quite different, more sinister meaning, as reflected in the German *Ohr-*

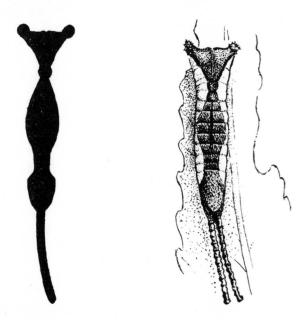

Caterpillar of the European puss moth (***Cerura vinula***). Actual length. c. 1 inch (25 mm).

wurm, the Russian *ukhovertka*, and many more, including Dutch and Swedish names, with a similar connotation. Just how far back the ear-entering belief can be traced I am unable to say with any certainty, but one apparent reference to it in a well-known English version of the first-century Roman writer Pliny's *Natural History* — that of Philemon Holland (1552–1637) — may be due merely to ever-free translation, or worse. According to Holland, Pliny says that 'if an earwig or such like vermin be gotten into the eare, make no more ado but spit into the same, and it will come forth anon'. Now obviously there have been many copyings and translations of classical works down the ages, but it seems that in all those Latin versions of Pliny available today the old natural historian makes no specific reference to earwigs at all, in this or any other context. He merely writes of using spittle as a means of getting small *animals* out of the ear: reasonably enough since, as mentioned earlier and elsewhere (page 87), if tiny insects *do* (occasionally) find their way into the ear, they are probably just as likely to be something other than earwigs. Did Holland impose his own perhaps borrowed prejudices on Pliny's writings and thus afford the phobia and the word 'earwig' a pedigree neither ever truly had?

In other animal names, it is our interpretation of them, rather than their etymology, that is in question. The large puss moth (*Cerura vinula*) and the smaller and more strongly patterned sallow kitten (*Furcula furcula*) and poplar kitten (*Furcula bifida*) moths are said to derive their names from a certain resemblance to the softly hairy flowers or *cat*kins of willows, sallows and poplars on whose foliage their caterpillars feed. In fact, the latter have equal claim to the origin of their feline designations. The newly-hatched, black larvae are themselves distinctly kittenish in appearance and the second-instar caterpillars even more so. Viewed from above, the latter's darker pattern, complete with 'ears' and tail, all delineated on a pale green or yellowish background, is astonishingly like the caricature of a Felix-type cat seated on its haunches with its back to the observer. The caterpillars have twin tails, but when held together, as they frequently are in repose, the effect is complete. Spread apart, as they tend to be when the larva is alarmed, we have that exemplar of happiness and self-satisfaction, a cat with two tails!

ANIMAL PLACE-NAMES

It is reasonable to assume that almost every country in the world has cities, towns and villages whose names indicate links with animals for which they are, or more usually were, especially noted. The past tense is, of course, particularly applicable to highly urbanised nations where the larger wild fauna has been pushed back or entirely ousted as the demand for human living space grew. In the United States, for example, the city of Buffalo is said to derive its name from the vast herds of bison that roamed the area in the early 1800s. Chicago's semantic origins are less obvious and lie, according to some authorities, in the Cree Indian name for the skunk, *sikak* (pronounced 'shikak').

Britain's place-names are of particular interest since that crowded land has lost more of its larger mammals than any other, and a variety of settlements, large and small, indicate the former presence of species long since vanished or even rendered extinct. In England, for example, wolves (*Canis lupus*) seem to have finally disappeared in the sixteenth century, but that they once roamed parts of the land in Saxon times is indicated by such names as Woolley, which occurs in counties as widely separated as Berkshire, Cambridgeshire and Yorkshire (West Riding), and in Hampshire's Woolmer (*wulf-mere*, or the lake where wolves drank). It is probable that these great wild dogs hung on longest in the bleak northern uplands and moorlands, notably in the North York Moors, where there are many place-names that point to man's interest in them. Some are Norman-French, deriving from the Saxons' eleventh-century conquerors, among them Louvenhowe and Loose Howes – from *loup*, wolf, *louve*, she-wolf, and *howe*, a barrow or burial-mound. The evocative-sounding Howl Moor is another Yorkshire locality whose name may well refer to past wolf presence. Old countrymen in the county's Upper Eskdale still apparently call midwinter 'T'howl time', which could refer either to the cries of hungry wolves or to human hunger, since *howl* also meant a topographical hollow, which might thus have been transferred, in a figurative sense, to imply hollow (empty) stomachs. By contrast, a number of what seem to be very obvious lupine place-names are nothing of the kind. Wolverhampton (Staffordshire) and Wolverton (Buckinghamshire) actually mean the farm (*tun*) of *Wulfrun* or *Wulfhere*, so that the adoption of the wolf's head emblem by the former town's famous football club is no more than a latter-day play on its name.

The European beaver (*Castor fiber*) is another species no longer living in Britain, but whose presence lives in certain place-names, notably at Beverley in South Yorkshire. The wild boar (*Sus scrofa*) finds similar commemoration at Everton (*eofor,* boar), a name which occurs in Bedfordshire, Nottinghamshire and Lancashire. Beavers seem to have become extinct in Britain by the twelfth century, the wild boar surviving for another five hundred years afterward.

That most majestic of birds, the golden eagle (*Aquila chrysaetos*), now has its principal British stronghold in the Highlands of Scotland, but it is likely that it roamed and nested far more widely in the past. Arnold (Old English *earn* or *erne*, eagle) in the West Riding of Yorkshire, and its namesake in Nottinghamshire's famous Sherwood Forest, probably indicate the birds' past presence much further south. Otters, too, now so much rarer than they were, are forever linked to Otterbourne (Hampshire), Otterburn (Northumberland) and Ottershaw (Surrey), as well as in Devon and Somerset's River Otter. That most English of mammals, the badger (*Meles meles*) found its nominal way into Bagshot (Surrey), Bagley (Berkshire, Shropshire, Somerset, West Riding of Yorkshire) and, via *broc*, the Old English name for the badger, in Brockham (Gloucestershire), Brockfield (Suffolk) and Brockenhurst (New Forest of Hampshire). Even insects find their niche, at Ampthill, in Bedfordshire: originally *ant*-hill (Anglo-Saxon *aemette-hyll*), in reference to the fact that the hamlet was notable for its ant-hills, probably the mounds of the wood-ant (*Formica rufa*), still present in the area.

Certain English place-names are intriguingly suggestive of the presence of mythical monsters, among them dragons (*draca*) at Drakelow (Bedfordshire, Derbyshire, Worcestershire) and Dragon's Hill, in Berkshire, where tradition has it England's patron saint, St George, fought his dragon – quite unjustifiably since the martyr was never in Britain. Great sea-serpents or worms (*wyrm*) seem to have been real enough to our ancestors to have prompted their commemoration in such places as Wormley (Hertfordshire) and Wormwood Scrubs, now the site of a famous London prison. At Filey, on Yorkshire's North Sea coast, the implicit reference is to a great sea monster (*fifel*), apparently sighted from its promontory (*eg*). Giants (*thyrs*) seem to have made their homes at Thursden (Lancashire) and Tusmore (Oxfordshire), while dwarfs (*dwerg*) could be located at Dwarriden, in the West Riding of Yorkshire, and elves (*elf*) at Elvedon (Suffolk) and Alveden (Lancashire)

EXTRACTS

Animals have supplied man with a whole range of useful products and extracts, although many of them bear names that give but small indication of their origins. Some, like *cat-gut*, are even downright misleading. Ailurophiles fearful of pet-snatchers will be relieved to know that cats play no part in providing the material so useful for making the strings of musical instruments and their bows, for weight suspension in grandfather clocks and for suturing or stitching wounds. It actually derives from the intestines of sheep or occasionally asses, mules and cattle. The name is said to be a corruption of *kit*-gut, a small fiddle or violin used by music and dancing masters (perhaps ultimately from *cithern*, another old stringed instrument, which doubtless required cat-gut), the 'kit' being subsequently confused with the same word for cat. It may even be that there is some deliberately jokey reference to the sounds made by less than fully competent strings-players, the implication being that their renderings were reminiscent of cats on the tiles.

Many marine animals yield obscurely-named materials. *Shagreen* is a kind of 'leather', generally made from the rough-surfaced belly-skin of various species of sharks and rays, used as an abrasive for polishing wood. It seems probable that the name derives from the same root as 'chagrin', suggestive of irritation or 'rubbing up the wrong way', such as one might a cat or in the incorrect use of one's shagreen.

Artists using *sepia*-tint may not always be aware that this dark brown, almost black, pigment originally came from the melanin-based 'ink' discharged for defensive purposes by species of cuttlefish (*Sepia*), whose much modified shells, commonly called cuttle-bone, are given to cage-birds, so that they can keep their beaks trimmed. Once used for writing purposes, the ink fades with age, which certainly cannot be said of an equally famous pigment (dye) called *Royal* or *Tyrian purple*, obtained from various Mediterranean whelks (*Murex* etc). The Phoenicians were specially noted exponents of the purple-dyeing industry, robes coloured with this most stable of dyes being an indication of rank in Ancient Roman times. 'Purple' itself derives from the Greek word for these dye-producing shellfish (*porphura*).

WORDS FROM THE CLASSICS

To the zoologist, the whole of an area's wild animal life constitutes its *fauna*, just as the plants are its flora. The term derives, as do many scientific and popular names, from classical mythology. *Faunus* was the old Roman god of all nature and country life in general, as was his Greek equivalent *Pan*, from whom we gain the prefix 'pan-', meaning 'all', as well as a more sinister connotation. Anyone in a panic was originally affected thus by the earthy god's voice or the sound of his pan-pipes. Faunus' or Pan's underlings were the lustful *fauns* and *satyrs*, which the vagaries of the English language have transformed into quite different modern applications – the one as the young fawns of deer, and the other into satire, which lays particular emphasis on lampooning the vices and follies of men (and satyrs).

Nymphs nowadays are attractive young girls, but originally were female demi-goddesses with which the Greeks peopled nature. The seas had their own particular nymphs, the oceanides and nereides; naiads were nymphs of rivers and streams, dryads and hamadryads those of trees, and oreades associated with mountains. Entomologically, nymph is today used for larvae of those insect groups which do not undergo full metamorphosis, such as dragonflies and crickets, those of the former being also called naiads because of their lengthy water life. The *larvae*

Apparently Hittite in origin, but a particular feature of Ancient Egyptian and Greek mythology, the sphinx was a fabulous beast with human head, wings, and the body and feet of a lion. (This particular design is from a piece of Rhodian pottery, probably late seventh century BC, now in the Pitt Rivers Museum, Oxford.)

themselves were originally the spirits or shades of the dead, as were the *lemures*, whose name is perpetuated in those large-eyed, long-fingered Old World primates, the lemurs, related to the monkeys, apes and man.

One group of sea-nymphs were the *sirens*, whose sweet song lured sailors to their doom. Today, their name is perpetuated in several ways: to indicate an alluring woman or a warning device, as well as in the scientific order Sirenia (the so-called 'sea-cows'). Another sea entity was *Cygnus*, son of Poseidon, the Greek god of the oceans. His name survives in the name we afford young swans, cygnets. The expression 'halcyon days', suggestive of calm, happy periods in one's life, finds its origin in Halcyone, the wife of Ceyx, who threw herself into the sea when her husband was drowned. In sympathy, the goddess Thetis changed both of them into birds, whose nest floated on the surface of the sea during the calmness of those days when the young were reared. *Halcyon* is today the generic name of some kingfishers, although they are, of course, associated principally with fresh waters: no bird could rear its young successfully on the sea's surface.

Certain words in our language betray evidence of our ancestors' fear of mythical monsters, currently softened into rather different meanings. The original *chimaera* was a fire-breathing, man-eating amalgam of a lion, goat and dragon, so impossible-sounding that it has now come to mean any fantastic vision or foolish fancy. The name is also applied to certain marine fishes related to the sharks and rays. The *sphinx* was equally fantastic. According to myth, it bore a woman's head and the body of a lion, and throttled all of those unable to answer a riddle it posed to them. The latter foible survives in the human physiologist's term for the muscle (sphincter) which controls the anal motions by relaxing and contracting. Anyone who adopts a sphinx-like attitude is silently inscrutable, while moths of the family *Sphingidae* (hawk-moths) are so-called because the apparently thoughtful, head-raised posture of their spike-tailed larvae when at rest recalls that of the original sphinx.

THE LANGUAGE OF SYMBOLS

Animal symbols are all around us. They occur in the flags or arms of nations and cities and noble families, as the devices of business concerns, of societies and clubs, in astrology, and in a host of other situations and connections. Sometimes they incorporate fabulous creatures, like the red dragon of Wales and the phoenix of fire insurance companies. Others are impossible hybrids or fanciful renderings of existing beings, among them the winged lion of St Mark and the Book of Revelation, the emblem of Venice at the height of her maritime power and influence, and the martlet, six of which form the centrepiece of the arms of the English county of Sussex, as representing those administrative areas established by the conquering Normans. Originally an imaginary bird, thought to have no legs, the martlet is clearly based on the swift or martin, since both are highly specialised aeronauts and the former, in fact, has such short legs, positioned far to the rear of its body, that it is quite unable to settle on the ground at all, just like the fourth, non-inheriting son of a noble lord, who also has a martlet as his device.

Other heraldic birds incorporate an element of fantasy. The pelican is commonly depicted 'vulning' or wounding her own breast to feed her young, originating from an ancient belief that is probably based on the reddish-yellow tint that white pelicans commonly assume about the neck during the breeding season. The eagle has been depicted with two heads, facing in opposite directions, since the days of the Hittites, and the symbol was also adopted by the Emperor Charlemagne (c. AD 742–814) and by the old Prussian, Austrian and Russian empires, perhaps to suggest their far-reaching extent. Albania's flag still incorporates the device today. Orthodox eagles headed the standards carried into battle by the Roman legions and occur in the flags of modern West Germany, Poland

and Spain, while the white-headed and 'bald' eagle (*Haliaeetus leuco-cephalus*), now sadly rare, is the impressive symbol of the United States of America. The eagle form of the church lectern or reading stand owes its origin, it seems, to the device of St John the Evangelist, one of the four writers of the gospels.

'National animals' can be either a true reflection of a country's indigenous fauna or, occasionally, spurious additions to it. The great grey kangaroo, black swan and piping shrike depicted in the armorial bearings of the Commonwealth of Australia are accurate enough; so, too, are the elephant of Thailand, the crocodile of Ancient Egypt (displayed on the coins of annexing Rome), the llama of Peru, the quetzal of Guatemala (also the country's unit of currency), the bird of paradise of Papua New Guinea, and the extinct dodo of Mauritius. On the other hand, the lion and leopards of the royal standard of England and Scotland are merely figurative borrowings, since neither has ever been part of the British fauna in historic times. Rather curiously, the Herald's Office leopard has only tenuous links with that of zoology, since blazonry makes no real distinction, it seems, between leopard and lion. Such a departure from fact appears to be linked to the original notion that the leopard was a cross between a lion (*leo*) and a panther (*pardel*), although the latter is, in reality, a melanic form of the leopard.

One of the most profitable sources for the collector of animal symbols is the inn sign. 'The Swan with Two Necks' is particularly worthy of note, since it is based on an artistic misunderstanding rather than the perpetuation of myth. Two *nicks* were the distinguishing mark of the Vintners' Company, applied to the birds' beaks during the Old English custom of swan-upping. Those birds belonging to the Dyers' Company were distinguished by a single nick, all the remaining swans on the River Thames belonging to the Crown and being by tradition left unmarked.

Medical practitioners will doubtless be aware that the worldwide symbol of their ancient profession is a snake coiled about a staff. The device is of extreme antiquity, and was originally that of Aesculapius, the Greek god of medicine, he in turn having obtained it, we are told, from Hermes, messenger and herald of the gods, whose staff, or *caduceus*, however bore *two* snakes. Long regarded as the personification of health and even immortality, certain snakes were, in ancient times, kept and tended in special temples devoted to Aesculapius and his daughter Hygeia (Greek) or Salus (Roman), from whose names, incidentally, we derive the healthful terms hygiene and salutary. A sacred snake coiled about a pedestal and fed from a patera (dish) by an attendant priest is a common reverse design on Roman Imperial coins. The emphasis on lengthy coiling and intertwining is perhaps not entirely fortuitous, since it is quite probable that a particular species was both kept and formed the

Reverse of an Athenian tetradrachm of the fifth century BC. The owl was the symbol of Pallas Athene, goddess of wisdom and the arts.

basis of the symbols concerned. The so-called Aesculapian snake (*Elaphe longissima*) is not merely among the longest species in Europe (up to 200 cm), but has a habit of climbing shrubs and trees in search of prey, which it kills by constriction and not with venom. It also practises a most curious 'combat dance' reminiscent of the entwined snake motif. When two rival males meet, they rush together, entwine their bodies together and rear up on their tails in a vertical position, making repeated lunges at each other: a spectacle tailor-made for the ancient symbol-seeker.

The popular linking of owls with wisdom probably owes its origin to another deific symbol. In Ancient Greece, the owl was the companion of Pallas Athene, goddess of wisdom, learning and artistic accomplishments, and was also depicted on the reverse of Athenian coins, popularly referred to as 'owls'. The little owl, active by both day and night and still common in southern Europe, seems a particularly likely candidate for the post of goddess-assistant, and its current scientific name, *Athene noctua*, perpetuates the connection.

Resurrection and immortality were themes close to the heart of ancient peoples, although one symbol suggestive of them will nowadays probably only be familiar to egyptologists. In Ancient Egypt the female African scarab-beetle's (*Scarabaeus sacer*) habit of rolling a ball of dung to a specially-prepared cavity as food for its larvae led to its representation as the symbol of the sun's perpetual rising and setting, of night and day, and consequently resurrection after death. Amulets showing the beetle with its ball of dung ('sun') held aloft between its forelegs, and friezes with the same motif, are among the most typical of Egyptian tomb embellishment and decoration. Insects' ability to totally transform themselves from one (larval) form into another quite different (adult) one rendered them

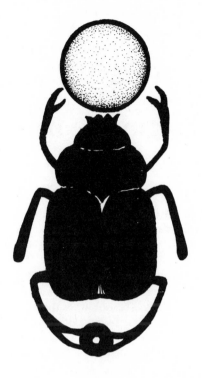

Scarab beetle symbol from an Ancient Egyptian papyrus box in the Pitt Rivers Museum, Oxford. The African scarab beetle (*Scarabaeus sacer*) was the symbol of the Egyptian sun-god Amon-Ra.

especially suitable subjects to apply to the human faith in *change* rather than death. In China, Indonesia, Mexico, Scandinavia, and many other countries, butterflies and cicadas are among those insects symbolically representative of immortality.

2·MISCONCEPTIONS AND HALF-TRUTHS

'RED RAG TO A BULL'

It is popularly supposed that a bull has only to be shown a red rag (or flag) or glimpse someone wearing clothing of this colour for it to 'see red' and charge full tilt at the offending item or person. Certainly, a bull merits respect, especially when in the company of a harem of cows, but it is doubtful if the aggressiveness it occasionally displays in such circumstances is any more than a response to what it probably considers an intrusion into its territory. The colour of the 'threat' would seem to be totally irrelevant. Indeed, the selection of red in this context is purely arbitrary: linked to our own traditional (psychological) ideas of red as being the colour of anger and danger, whereas other colours, like blue and green, are generally considered more 'restful'.

Zoologists and animal psychologists still debate as to the extent that the higher animals see or interpret colours, in comparison with the way that humans do. Most are agreed that cattle and many other mammals have only a limited appreciation of colour and may see their surroundings only in black and white and in varying shades of grey. This may even be so when (as in our bull) the eye contains a good proportion of $cones_1$: those structures which, in human eyes, are primarily concerned with colour perception and differentiation; for there are, in fact, different types of cones, each concerned with the interpretation of colours of different wavelengths. As a result, an animal may 'see' and recognise one colour but not another, and perhaps not distinguish, say, red from blue, except in terms of how much light these colours reflect. Domestic animals like dogs and cats are now thought to have some faint perception of colour differences, although it is not always clear what it is the animal is responding to when it appears to recognise and distinguish varyingly coloured items. A dog may unerringly pick out a can of its favourite tinned food from a batch of others, but even if its subtle olfactory senses were not at work – and a dog's sense of smell is many times superior to ours – it is quite probably recognising the label's pattern and not its colour as such.

People, too, share with other animals an inability to recognise certain colours, even though their vision may otherwise be normal and their eyes possess both cones (for colour vision) and rods (for light perception and acuity of image). Such colour-blindness apparently lies in the absence or malfunction of those cones concerned with the recognition of particular colours. Significantly, when compared with our original bull, the most frequently encountered condition is a lack of distinction between red and green, which the colour-blind individual may confuse with yellow-brown or grey, respectively.

SEEING IN THE DARK

As their owners will know, domestic cats are as much, if not more, at home after dark as they are during the day. Their activity and agility scarcely impaired by the gloom, they hunt, court, fight rival toms or just slink about 'seeing what they can see' in a way that must have seemed particularly mysterious and even uncanny to our occult-conscious ancestors. Given this, it is natural that we should think of cats and other basically nocturnal animals as being able actually to see in the dark – an impression heightened by the way their eyes glow like live coals when they catch the glare of a torch or car headlight. The fact is, however, that no animal can see properly in *total* darkness. Cats, badgers, foxes, and a host of other night creatures, certainly see very much better in dim light than we do, but there must be some available light, however slight, for them to determine the shape and general nature of such objects or creatures as they encounter. The first thing that has to be said is that nocturnal animals have a great many more light-gathering rod cells in the retinas of their eyes than we do, but in addition many of them possess a most efficient means of making the very most of such light as is present in the form of a layer of flinty crystals behind the retina, called a *tapetum*. This, as it were, gives the eye a second chance by reflecting back such light as was initially missed by the retina's photoreceptors and absorbed in the general tissues of the eye. As a result, the retina is able to send a greatly reinforced image-signal to the brain, all being effected at lightning speed. It is, of course, the tapetum layer that gives the glowing effect mentioned earlier.

One of the interesting things about the eyes of nocturnal animals lies in the shape of their *iris,*: that structure which regulates the amount of light taken in by the eye. In cats, foxes, badgers, and many snakes and lizards, the iris is elliptical and not round as in man and other basically diurnal animals. The difference seems to be linked to the possession of a tapetum, since the elliptical iris can close rather more fully than a round one and thus prevent its possessor being temporarily blinded when caught in strong sunlight or in a sudden flash of light after dark. Examination of a cat's eyes directly after such illumination will reveal the iris closed to the narrowest of slits. Cats need only about one-sixth of the light our eyes require in order to see properly, although they do not have things all their own way in visual terms. What they gain in overall perception after dark they lose in acuity – that is, in the sharpness and three-dimensional nature of items seen. To balance this, however, the feline's senses of hearing and smell are extremely acute, as is its touch, aided by sensitive facial whiskers.

OSTRICH ODDITIES

The hoary old notion that the flightless ostrich (*Struthio camelus*) will hide its head in the sand rather than face up to danger has found a permanent place in our language to suggest someone who deliberately avoids a confrontation or reality. The most usual explanation offered for this lovely bit of nonsense is that it is based on the attitude assumed by the hen ostrich when brooding her huge eggs. Whilst engaged in this passive activity, she instinctively extends her long neck in front of her, below the level of her rounded body, so that all that is visible from a distance is an apparently inanimate, greyish hummock. Sitting upright, with head raised, on her precious cargo, she would be far more conspicuous to predators like jackals and wild dogs, whose principal target would probably be the eggs, since full-grown ostriches make formidable adversaries. One interesting point here is that while egg-brooding duties are shared by cock and hen, the drably-coloured female assumes day duty, whereas the more strikingly patterned, black and white cock takes over at night, when his appearance is less likely to attract attention. This, however, is only part of the 'head in the sand' story, for ostriches also take up a head-lowered, myth-conducive posture on other occasions, sometimes seated on their forwardly-articulating 'knees', with the head directed inwards between the legs, as if checking that everything is in order! Even their everyday foraging for food – low-growing vegetation, lizards and insects – might well produce the fabulous impression.

Ostriches' feeding habits have given rise to another popular myth, to the effect that these extraordinary birds will eat virtually anything, prompting cartoonists to depict ostriches with bottles and other unlikely objects halfway down their long necks. While clearly exaggerated, the belief conceals an element, at least, of the truth. Ostriches enjoy healthy appetites, but they appear to have (literally) little or no taste and indeed cannot afford to be choosy in their relatively unproductive plains terrain. They are certainly known to swallow large amounts of sand, grit and small stones, apparently to aid digestion, and also display a tendency to snap up and swallow a miscellany of other, larger items. Like crows, they appear to find metal objects particularly attractive, more especially if they are bright and glittering. Various fiction writers have made amusing use of this theme, notably H.G. Wells in his short story 'A Deal in Ostriches', wherein one of a group of the birds is thought to have swallowed a valuable diamond.

ELEPHANTS, MICE AND MEMORY

Accustomed as we are to seeing elephants in zoos and safari parks, it is easy to forget how strange and terrifying these huge and uniquely impressive beasts must have seemed to ancient peoples encountering them for the first time. They certainly caused considerable dismay and confusion in the ranks of the Romans when they first appeared in the armies of Pyrrhus, King of Epirus (famous for his 'Pyrrhic victories') in the third century BC; and they have also been used to good effect, both in warfare and for transport, by the Carthaginian Hannibal and by the old Indian princes, for example.

The problem with elephants in the fraught situations of battle is that they are often rather less steady under fire than horses. They are liable to panic, causing as many problems to their own side as to the enemy. Just what triggers off such reactions, apart from justifiable sheer fright, it is not easy to say, but it is unlikely to be mice, despite the belief that elephants have an innate fear of a mammal at the other extreme of the size scale. Tests have been carried out by releasing mice and rats, including more conspicuous white ones, into elephants' enclosures, but the great beasts ignored them even when they ran over their feet. What they *did* react to, it seems, was the sound made by the mice rustling through paper and hay, this immediately setting the nearest elephant trumpeting, the chorus being subsequently joined in by its fellows. One is forced to wonder if this might suggest to them the crackling outbreak of fire, coupled with their inability to see properly what is going on beneath their great bodies. Elephants' sight is not very good at the best of times, so it is probable that quite minor ground disturbances could set them off on a stampede.

Whether elephants have a better memory than other animals, originating the long-standing belief that they never forget a friend or injury, is something of a moot point. Investigations involving testing their mental powers suggest there may be at least something in it. One five-year-old taught to recognise complicated designs remembered them clearly a year later; it also recalled musical notes and even simple melodies more than eighteen months afterward. Clearly, there are practical difficulties involved in testing the true extent of animals' memories – the time element itself, for example – but it would be interesting to know if there are records of zoo-keepers or mahouts renewing acquaintance with elephants after many years. Would a young elephant, for example, recognise the man it knew as a boy when it approached the end of its life (which rarely extends beyond seventy years, not over a hundred as is commonly believed)? In this connection, it is perhaps worth noting that the elephant's gestation period is considerably more than twice that of man's and the calves' lactation extends over several years. Since they take so long to grow, they might be equally slow in forgetting!

One item of pachyderm lore that seems to be purest fancy, despite wide currency in Africa and parts of Asia, is that elephants have special graveyards, to which they wander when they feel death nearing. Having said that, elephants do seem to show a certain interest in their dead, just as do certain other mammals (page 59). One elephant cow was seen to carry her dead calf on her tusks for several days, displaying every indication of sorrow, before scraping a hollow beneath a tree and burying it. Others have been observed to combine to inter dead members of their herd beneath a layer of leaves and branches or even, quite inexplicably, deliberately disperse the bones of those elephant skeletons they encounter.

SNAKE-CHARMERS

It can scarcely be doubted that much of the mystique surrounding the popular image of the Oriental snake-charmer owes its perpetuation to the widespread fear and loathing with which snakes in general are regarded. The point becomes clear if we, as it were, set the scene at a typical exposition of this age-old tourist attraction and examine its various aspects in more detail. With the audience (conveniently) positioned at a respectful distance, the Indian or perhaps Egyptian exponent squats in front of his snake-basket and, by playing on his pipe, which he gently oscillates to and fro, induces the reptile to slowly unwind, rear up and then sway in time to the music. The whole procedure looks highly dramatic, convincing and dangerous but in fact it owes its effect to certain tricks of the trade which are carefully withheld and concealed from the cringing public. Firstly, it is pretty certain that many of the snakes used are harmless, non-venomous species. But even in cases where deadly hooded cobras are involved there is rarely any danger of player or watchers being bitten since the snake's fangs have usually either been removed or blocked with wax; sometimes its jaws are carefully sewn up. What is more, the snake is prevented from wriggling

Snake-charming.

away and thus causing panic because its tail is secured by tape at the bottom of the basket. No wonder the charmer feels able to add the final, daring touch to the ritual by bestowing a kiss on his much imposed-upon partner in deception!

The perpetrator of all this blatant sham is generally safe from exposure, since few members of the public are likely to wish to check the points mentioned. In any case, the whole concept of snake-charming is based on a false premise, for the plain fact is that snakes are almost totally deaf, at least to airborne vibrations. They can pick up and respond to tremors received via the ground but because they possess no eardrums their appreciation of music is not merely minimal: it is non-existent. Thus the snake's initial rearing up out of its basket is not in response to the piper's seductive melody but because, having been kept in darkness for some time, its natural reaction is to spiral sunwards. When it sways its head and fore-body from side to side, it is merely following the movements of the pipe, some say as it would when confronting another member of its species during territorial challenge.

One of the snakes most commonly used by the snake-charmer is the Egyptian spectacled cobra (*Naja haje*). This was almost certainly the 'asp' used by Cleopatra to effect her suicide, which she is said to have preferred rather than to fall into the hands of Augustus after the defeat of her lover Mark Antony in 31 BC. 'Asp' was a term used for any poisonous snake in ancient times and must not be confused with the so-called asp viper (*Vipera aspis*), which is confined to southern Europe and does not occur as an indigenous species in Africa. This apart, vipers are scarcely the most appropriate snakes for use by potential suicides since while their bites and venom are exceedingly painful they are rarely fatal. Cobras, on the other hand, kill quickly and were in Ancient Egypt regularly offered as a means of self-destruction to political prisoners, so that they might escape less honourable methods of execution. The veneration with which snakes were regarded by the Egyptians is indicated by the fact that many of their divinities and pharaohs (including Cleopatra herself) wore a special serpent head-dress, incorporating what is clearly a representation of a threatening cobra. The device was called *uraeus*, a word which derives from the Greek and ultimately Egyptian, meaning a cobra or asp.

For centuries, snakes were thought to have the evil eye, with an ability to fascinate and lure potential human and animal victims to their doom. The notion is perhaps most popularly highlighted in Rudyard Kipling's *Jungle Book*, wherein the boy Mowgli is strictly enjoined not to look the great python, Kaa, directly in the eye, for fear of being rendered immobile and helpless. The idea presumably arose from the snake's unwinking stare (it has no eyelids) and its method of stalking prey, this being for the most part effected slowly and deliberately, the snake keeping its gaze fixed on its intended victim and often gently swaying its head from side to side, while its target is still trying to decide whether the slight movement constitutes a threat or no. It has been suggested that with distinctively marked snakes the potential victim's attention may be focussed on some particular part of the aggressor's pattern, such as the dark blotches on top of the European viper's head, and become sufficiently 'fascinated' by it as to lose all sense of approaching danger. Even to human observers, snakes are commonly so beautifully and disruptively camouflaged that it takes a while for the eye to distinguish the shape of the animal as a whole, so that one's fixed attention during their contemplation *might* give another person the impression that some kind of hypnotism was taking place.

Another ancient belief which has found its way into symbolism to suggest the concept of infinity is that snakes commonly progress by tucking their tails in the mouth and bowling themselves along like a hoop. It is, of course, absolute nonsense, yet I have a record of a lady writing to a popular natural history magazine some seventy years ago and affirming that she *and her husband* had actually witnessed a snake advancing towards them in this manner. It is difficult to know quite how to regard such palpable misobservations, except as deliberate hoaxes or (in this particular case) some form of collective hallucination induced by already firmly-held belief, since the notion is based on a physical impossibility. Snakes commonly rest in a tight, flat circle, wound up rather like a watchspring, but that is about the nearest they ever get to the mythical 'tail-in-the-mouth' position. Neither do snakes ever progress in vertical loops, like the caterpillars of Geometrid moths or the fabulous sea-serpent (page 134).

One widely-held belief about snakes that merits closer attention and analysis, despite the derision with which it tends to be regarded by most herpetologists, is that they will take up their young in their mouth or even deliberately swallow them during times of danger. As recently as 1979 a man told of seeing this happen on Bookham Common, in Surrey: a large adder, disturbed by the group's approach, gaping wide and allowing three tiny young ones to enter her mouth. A whole host of somewhat similar sightings are on record from earlier years, although it is not always clear whether it is mouth-retention that is being referred to or the more drastic total engorgement. The famous 'Brusher' Mills who during a lifetime spent in the New Forest of Hampshire (he died in 1905) caught some 30,000 snakes, including 5,000 adders, swore that he had seen adders 'swallow' their young on hundreds of occasions.

So far as I am aware there is no scientifically authenticated case of snakes protecting their progeny by temporarily retaining them in their mouths, but that is not to say it does not happen. Various fish, such as the guppy, actually brood their young in the mouth, and the Nile crocodile habitually allows hers to use her death-trap of a mouth as a snug retreat. It is therefore possible that snakes might occasionally do the same, providing the young were not too numerous – although even here it is worth noting that snakes can actually dislocate their lower jaw when swallowing large prey, which ploy might thus be used to the effect under discussion. That is one thing. Actual ingurgitation is quite another and might be effected for totally different reasons. Many animals, ranging from doe rabbits to semi-social earwigs, will actually eat their young if disturbed too soon after their birth and if this did happen in snakes swallowing whole would be the only way they could manage it, since their teeth are not designed for mastication but only for prey seizure and retention. Cannibalism of the young of other individuals is certainly well attested in some species of snakes, more especially where protein-hungry females with developing embryos of their own are concerned.

Such a thesis could well fit a good many of the observations of snakes swallowing their own offspring. (The oft-quoted suggestion that the baby snakes merely *seem* to disappear by hiding beneath their parent's body is unlikely to answer more than a minority of cases.) Unfortunately, the whole issue has become clouded by an ignorance of snake physiology. Many people have attested to finding young live snakes in an adult female adder's body after it had been killed and cut open, offering it as proof of (protective) swallowing, which it most decidedly is not. The point here is that the adder, like many other snakes, produces its young fully formed, though still enclosed in an easily ruptured amniotic membrane; so that finding a female with live little ones inside her is usually merely an indication that she was about to give birth. A good many years ago a natural history magazine carried an account of purported young-swallowing by a Texan rattlesnake which demonstrates precisely this point and the dangers of taking things at face value. Having killed the snake, one of the party placed his foot on its body and exerted pressure on it, working his way towards the head. To the observers' astonishment, three or four tiny live rattlesnakes emerged from the mother's mouth. Since we know that birth is via the vent and not the mouth, could this be proof of young-swallowing for protective purposes? Not at all. All that had happened is that undue pressure on the parent's body had ruptured the membraneous wall between the ovaries and stomach, thus forcing the young to emerge by an uncustomary route.

To complicate matters still further, there is also the possibility of cannibalistic snakes disgorging recently-taken prey which prove to be still alive. This sort of reaction not uncommonly occurs when snakes are

The European adder or viper (**Vipera berus**).

42

handled, and while the vomited victims are usually already dead (more particularly, of course, where venomous species are concerned), victims are retained in the gullet for a short period before being transferred and subjected to digestion in the stomach, and could survive there for a while in a semi-comatose condition. Many years ago, I was given a clear demonstration of this point after a (non-venomous) grass snake I had brought home reacted to my excessive handling by disgorging a small male toad. After a few moments' passivity, during which the fortunate amphibian lay with its eyes closed and deeply withdrawn into their sockets, it slowly stirred itself and then ambled away as if nothing had happened. As I have said, this sort of thing could easily happen with snakes cannibalising other snakes, even with venomous species. Adders and other poisonous snakes inject variable amounts of venom into their victims and might even withhold it altogether in certain circumstances.

SNAKE-KILLERS AND PRICKLY DEFENCES

It is often maintained that animals that habitually prey on venomous snakes, among them mongooses (the correct plural), of which there are about fifty species, with a distribution that ranges from the Far East to Africa, the Middle East and southern Iberia, are immune to their venom. These attractive but fierce little mammals certainly have a high tolerance of snake toxins and appear to become increasingly immune after successive bites, rather as do human snake handlers. For the most part, however, it is their amazing reflexes, agility and sharp eyesight which keep them out of trouble when facing their dangerous foes, since there are records of mongooses dying from snake bite. Strikes of cobras and puff adders can be lightning-fast, but the mongoose is generally able to avoid them until it sees the chance of darting in and seizing its adversary behind the neck and severing its spinal cord, clinging on grimly the while, despite often being buffeted and bruised by the reptile's violent thrashings. Rudyard Kipling's famous story 'Rikki-Tikki-Tavi' (a name based on the mongoose's chittering cry) incorporates a vivid account of just such a duel.

Mongooses have been kept as household pets and pest-controllers in India and parts of Africa, notably Egypt, for probably thousands of years. The Roman writer Martial records that ladies of his day (first century AD) were particularly fond of their pet mongooses, which they and the Ancient Egyptians called ichneumons. The Egyptians raised their own particular species (*Herpestes ichneumon*) to deity level, at least partly because of its snake-killing proficiency and the ease with which it found and consumed the eggs of dangerous crocodiles.

The European hedgehog (*Erinaceus europaeus*) is another mammal that kills and eats snakes, although the reptiles probably do not figure very highly in its diet. By contrast with the mongoose, hedgehogs are clumsy movers and their defence against the strikes of venomous snakes, principally adders, tends to be of a somewhat passive kind. Covered as it is with a mass of tough, specially modified hairs, arranged in a complicated criss-cross fashion, the hedgehog merely tucks in its head and legs and receives the adder's strikes on its spines, those along its sides and in front of the head being erectile. Then, when the reptile has exhausted itself by repeated lunges and perhaps has damaged its mouth against the prickly defence, the hedgehog rolls on its prey and seizes and kills it in much the same way that the mongoose does. Hedgehog fatalities from snake bite are known, especially in young 'urchins', but it is apparently more usual for them to be merely a bit off-colour for a while, with an accompanying swelling of the wound, which often tends to be on their rather vulnerable nose. Like mongooses, hedgehogs seem to be able to build up some sort of immunity to venom after successive bites of a fairly mild nature.

Prickly defences of a rather different character are possessed by the porcupine, a type of rodent, which exists in various species in Africa, South-East Asia, the Americas and (one species) southern Europe. Old stories of porcupines being able actually to discharge or shoot their quills when threatened are legion and not so much false as over-accentuated. The quills certainly cannot be used as projectiles, but many of them are so loosely attached, as well as erectile, as to be easily discarded and thus form an unlooked-for and highly unpleasant mouthful for anything attacking their possessor. Conducting its defence by means of backward rushes, the porcupine increases the effect of its spiky defence by a powerful lashing of tail and body, which may result in the spines being driven deep into the aggressor's skin. The quills do not contain venom, as is widely believed, although they bear a series of barbs at the tips which make them difficult to extract and may induce secondary infection. There have been many fatalities among predators, such as bears and mountain lions, which have been unwise enough to attack a porcupine, not merely through infection of the wound but from the spines working into the body and piercing some vital organ.

FOX CUNNING

While foxes today are becoming increasingly opportunistic in raiding town refuse bins and even rearing litters in suburban back gardens, most tales of their astuteness derive from old countrymen, notably those who have observed their methods of avoiding huntsmen. One that has stood the test of time, and is still stoutly championed, tells of their alleged way of ridding themselves of fleas and lice. According to this ancient belief, the fox first collects a quantity of sheep's wool, perhaps from a barbed wire fence; then, holding the wool in its mouth, it backs very slowly into a pond, lake or stream until eventually only the wool and the tip of the fox's nose are above water. The theory is, of course, that in order to escape drowning the parasites are driven ever upwards by the fox's increasing inundation until they have all taken refuge in the wool. Then, having achieved its purpose, the fox simply releases the now flea-crowded wool, letting it glide away downstream, before making its way to the bank.

It is a charming notion and one I would love to believe. Unfortunately, though, it betrays ignorance of the nature of both fox and fleas. First of all, it is unlikely that the fox would be completely drenched to the skin by its immersion. Just as in most domestic dogs, its outer layer of guard hairs is somewhat greasy, which has the effect of preventing the skin and under-fur from being wetted to any great degree. Leaving the water, a fox (or dog) has merely to give itself a vigorous shake for it to be virtually dry again. But even should the fox's largely waterproof coat *not* prevent water getting to the fleas, it is extremely doubtful if the latter would readily abandon their host in the way suggested, if at all. Their reaction would almost certainly be to cling all the harder to hair and skin, probably closing their air-breathing holes (spiracles) until the flood had abated. Just about the only thing really guaranteed to make a flea leave home is if its living host dies and thus cuts off its source of blood food.

TANGLED TOADS

In this supposedly highly educated day and age, some of the persisting beliefs about animals and their behaviour seem astonishingly naive. Only a few years ago, for example, I was showing an averagely intelligent Derbyshire lady a colony of breeding toads when she suddenly asked me if it were true that the young toads were deliberately strangling the old. It is an ancient belief, but one that I had fondly believed had long since died the death. The true explanation of the springtime activity we were mutually contemplating was that the 'young' toads were really males and the larger ones females, such disparity of size being quite common in the animal world. During mating, the little male clasps his matronly partner about the body, usually behind the forelegs or sometimes around the neck, until the latter voids her eggs, which he then fertilises externally with his sperm. There is thus no direct mating, or copulation, as such. The males' grip is astonishingly tight and there is frequently so much milling about and thrashing of the water during the early stages of courtship that I suppose one might excuse those with an absolutely

A pair of albino common frogs (***Rana temporaria***) in amplexus.

minimal knowledge of natural history for assuming that some sort of toad pogrom were taking place!

The strange thing is that there is an element of truth in the implication that the female toads are, in some way, at risk during the hurly-burly of mating. Normal one-to-one sexual encounters present no problems for either partner, of course, but complications arise when, as frequently happens, there are far more male toads in a typical pond breeding site than females. Such imbalances of the sexes are common in nature, since they ensure that no female remains unmated – theoretically, at least. In the toads' case, there is thus considerable competition among the males for a plump partner and rivals are not even deterred when a male has beaten them to it and already seized the female in the amplexus position. Other males may cling to other parts of her body: undersides, legs, in fact anywhere they can reach. The result is frequently a veritable 'knot' of toads (the noun of aggregation for these amphibians), the female often being almost hidden by clinging, would-be partners, so much so as to render fertilisation a virtual impossibility. More significantly, such an excess of amorous interest by the males often results in the female being, quite literally, smothered or strangled – which takes us back to where we started.

Outside the breeding season, toads are terrestrial, spending the day in some subterranean retreat and emerging at night to hunt for worms and insects. In winter they hibernate, passing into a coma-like state, when

46

their respiratory rate falls to the very minimum needed to maintain the spark of life. Often they squeeze themselves into some small crevice, perhaps beneath a wall for this purpose. It goes without saying that toads do not feed during their winter sleep, although there is clearly a very low rate of breakdown of the body's fatty tissues to provide energy for respiration and breathing, the latter so shallow as to be almost imperceptible, the heart-beat being also greatly slowed down. Since all amphibians (toads, frogs, newts and salamanders), as well as reptiles, are poikilothermic or 'cold-blooded', their body temperature more or less adjusts itself to that of their surroundings. There are records of toads and frogs surviving being frozen solid in ice, though generally only for limited periods of time. Desert-living toads are also capable of subsisting deep in the sub-soil for about a year until seasonal rains spark off their emergence and breeding.

The toad's ability to survive total entombment, cut off from a direct air-supply and, of course, lacking food, was in the past the subject of much scientific controversy, many people having attested to finding live toads sealed within blocks of stone, perhaps in the foundation of a building, the assumption being that the animals had managed to survive there for several years. The indefatigable investigator William Buckland (1784–1856) long ago demonstrated that toads can exist for about a year sealed in porous limestone, but not two, and that more impervious material, hardening or settling after initial commandeering, proved a literal death-trap.

IMPOSSIBLE GIANTS

The popular tendency to exaggerate the size of animals, encountered or not, has been taken to particularly nonsensical lengths in literature and films. Insects and spiders, for example, are regularly introduced as having grown to man-size, or greater, perhaps as the result of atomic radiation or experiment. The theme is an absolute non-starter, for a variety of reasons. Unlike mammals, which are able to attain a greater (though always limited) size because of an internal framework of bone and cartilage, the insect's 'skeleton' is external and fixed and incapable of expansion once the animal has attained adulthood, since it consists of a dead material called chitin. Whereas, too, vertebrate animals possess a most efficient means of circulating energy-releasing oxygen by means of the blood, conveyed to all parts of the body by veins and capillaries, the insect's respiratory system is designed to work over much shorter distances. It breathes via a system of tubes (tracheae) which open to the surface as small air-holes (spiracles) along the sides of its body. Air travels along these passages by simple conduction, unaided by blood (which in insects is used principally for transporting food and waste matter), and is then dispersed to all parts of the body by minute tracheoles. Conduction is at best a rather slow business and becomes increasingly inefficient the greater the distance and area that needs to be covered; it is also rendered still more sluggish during cold conditions, when the air is denser.

Facts like these make it clear that our hypothetical giant insect (or spider, for the same principles apply to all arthropods) would be at a considerable disadvantage on several counts. Borne down by vastly increased atmospheric pressure, its outer armour, so useful in normal circumstances, would become a dead weight, rendering it rather like a mediaeval knight without a charger to ride! The energy required to propel such a living 'ironclad' would be totally lacking, since while admittedly the giant's spiracles and tracheae would be proportionately that much larger, its volume would have increased at a far greater rate than its surface area. To get going at all, our potentially fearsome insect titan's respiration rate would have to speed up enormously – and that would not work either since air is only conducted at a fixed rate. Even should it be created in the first place, such an insect would quickly die and present no threat to man or anything else while alive.

Nature has, in the past, experimented with insects much larger than any in existence today, but they were giants only in the relative sense, and even here appearances can be deceptive. Much of the size of those giant dragonflies, some 2 feet (60 cm) across the wings, that zoomed over the Carboniferous swamps some 300 million years ago, went into length, as distinct from all-round bulk, just as it does with present-day dragonflies.

With bodies bearing spiracles down their entire length, the thinness of such groups clearly reduces the problems of respiration; moreover, a dragonfly's wings are merely inanimate appendages, operated by muscles attached to the thorax. A few tropical beetles, such as the African goliath and the South American *Titanus giganteus*, are admittedly both relatively bulky and heavy, but they are still no more than about 6 inches (15 cm) long and very far from typical in a world which dictates that, so far as insects are concerned, small is best.

To be fair to modern fantasists, the theme of giant insects is far from being a totally modern conceit. The fourteenth-century traveller Sir John Mandeville (who some consider to be himself fictional) told of seeing ants in Ceylon as big as cats, apparently guarding 'hills of gold' and capable of killing and devouring men. Earlier writers refer to even larger ants in the mountains of India and the deserts of Arabia which were also, it seems, mining gold. Such curious beliefs are perhaps more revealing of the human character than anything else, in reflecting a combination of man's insatiable cupidity with a respect for ants' industry.

INTRUSIVE SPIDERS

The dislike that many people have of spiders, which can sometimes assume phobia proportions (page 78), is scarcely improved by their tendency to occur in houses and, more especially, lurk in the bath or hand-basin. Their apparent reluctance or inability to get out again suggests that they have made their way in via the waste-pipe and plug-hole, but this is not so. Modern western plumbing makes such mountaineering feats impossible since the system includes a virtually impassable U-bend, and spiders cannot swim. This feature also makes it difficult for the hard-hearted to swill the intruder away by what they think is the way it came in. Always provided the plug is not inserted, the spider can usually make its escape upward by tucking in its legs, closing its breathing spiracles, and letting its natural buoyancy bring it to the surface again, the climb back into the bath via the inner surface of the pipe being perhaps less difficult than it would be up the smoother, sloping sides of the bath itself. Spiders have tiny claws at the tips of their legs which help them to get a purchase on any irregularity of a surface, which is why they can climb walls or even ceilings, if not glass or enamel.

Spiders found in the bath were almost certainly in the house already before they became, as it were, marooned. They could well have arrived via its sides or dropped in from the ceiling, any fall from height presenting no problem to them since all spiders are able to abate its force by the use of safety lines of silk extruded from terminal spinnerets. The reason they come in the first place is straightforward enough. Spiders are thirsty creatures and need moisture, not least since their bodies are prone to desiccation. With this object in mind, they simply 'follow their noses' – present only in the form of sensitive mouth-palps which assume the role of insects' antennae.

In popular folklore, spiders embody the age-old adage about the female of the species being deadlier than the male, which is in many cases no more than the plain unvarnished truth. It would be untrue to say that female spiders invariably kill and eat their male partners, whether before, during or after mating, but the latter certainly have to watch their step, at least partly because they are commonly smaller and weaker and could easily be mistaken for prey when they invade their beloved's home web. In consequence, male spiders employ a variety of stratagems in order to approach a potential partner with greater safety, ranging from the use of special signals, principally waving of their specially enlarged palps, and (at a respectful distance) tweaking strands of the female's web, to deliberately tying her down with silk. Sometimes 'presents', consisting of silk-wrapped insects, are offered to the female to distract her attention while he fertilises her – the latter in itself a curious business, since it involves no copulation, as such, but the insertion of his previously sperm-

49

charged palps into her epigyne. Probably most of those males that fall victim to protein-hungry females have become exhausted by successive matings. Many male spiders scarcely feed at all once they come to maturity, but spend the whole of their brief lives making increasingly hazardous visits to one female after another, until eventually their luck runs out. Paradoxically, it is occasionally the male's small size that constitutes his best defence against cannibalism, since it enables him to evade his mistress' jaws. In some species the male is so minute as scarcely to constitute a worthwhile meal, notably in tropical *Nephila*, where the male is about a thousandth of the enormous female in size and weight.

SURVIVING MUTILATION

The ability of animals to survive mutilation, perhaps the loss of a limb or even complete bisection of the body, has long been the subject of popular speculation, more especially where cold-blooded animals, such as earthworms, are concerned. Many a gardener, having neatly if inadvertently severed a worm with his spade, must have felt it probable that the two halves would not only heal their wounds but even take up an independent existence, principally because of their continued convulsive wriggling and an apparent lack of clearly defined head. The truth is rather different. Straightforward bisection of a worm will almost certainly result in death for both halves, but an inch or so removed from the worm's narrower tail end, leaving the anterior part (containing the head, primitive heart, brain and digestive system) intact, does not invariably prove fatal. What *never* happens is for the severed (tail) section to take up a separate life of its own, although the strange thing is that this sort of thing can and does happen in still more primitive animals. Certain flatworms (*Planaria*) display quite astonishing powers of regeneration, being able not merely to survive as separate individuals after being cut in two but form completely new worms from minute pieces cut from the original.

Such extreme powers of recovery decrease the more specialised, asymmetrical and decentralised an animal becomes, and in many groups the ability is lost when full adult growth is attained. Larval insects can grow a new limb if one is lost, but it is commonly smaller than the original and, in any case, is only replaceable during changes of the whole cuticle. Adult insects, spiders, harvestmen, and so forth, are quite unable to replace lost appendages. Vertebrates are not very good at limb regeneration, either, although amphibians, such as newts, may re-grow not just one toe from the stump of a lost one but two, often branched at the tip like the antler of a deer.

DO COLD-BLOODED ANIMALS FEEL PAIN?

Physiologically, the extent to which any animal feels pain or distress is exceedingly difficult to assess. We can observe responses to hurt or chart the electro-chemical impulses sent by pain receptors in the afflicted parts to the brain, but this tells us little about how the animal actually *feels* in such circumstances. Even in man, pain is a highly subjective phenomenon and one person's level of toleration may be greater or less than another's, perhaps linked to character and mental attitude. The lower animals seem particularly insensitive to pain, if their reactions to drastic mutilation are anything to go by. Insects with their abdomen completely severed will probably not survive long for purely physiological reasons, but while they live appear to feel no discomfort and continue feeding, apparently quite unconcerned about anything else, while the ingested food simply oozes out of the gaping posterior cavity.

In popular parlance, of course, sensitivity to pain is closely linked to whether an animal is warm- (or hot-) or cold-blooded (that is, whether it can regulate its own body temperature or has to rely on ambient temperatures). Indeed, both terms have found their way into the language to suggest widely differing temperaments. Just as someone who is apparently totally lacking in sensitivity and emotion is cold-blooded (French *sang-froid*), so are animals of this type thought to be completely unmoved by pain, pleasure or any other human emotion. It is on this basis that anglers tend to justify their activity by maintaining that the fish they hook, and the worms and 'gentles' they use as bait, are cold-blooded and thus insensitive to the indignities imposed on them. The matter is difficult to prove either way. What *is* certain is that the fish are in distress from at least one cause, since they have been taken from their natural environment, in which they are adapted to breathe water-dissolved air (by means of gills), into a totally alien one. In this sense, at least, angling is cruel and the fish undoubtedly sensitive to pain.

3·ANTHROPOMORPHISM – OR IS IT?

RAT TALES

Whether it is their communal way of living or age-old conflict with man that has sharpened their wits, I cannot say, but there is no doubt that rats are among the most adaptable and successful of all the mammals, despite every human endeavour to eradicate them. That they are genuinely intelligent seems beyond doubt, which makes it no accident that rats are among those animals most frequently kept by students of animal behaviour. Displaying a far from inconsiderable ability to actually reason things out when faced with new and unusual problems, laboratory rats learn to negotiate the most complicated labyrinths and operate food-release systems with remarkable rapidity, and may even experience a small but significant enlargement of the brain as a result of having to cope with such difficulties.

Wild rats, not surprisingly, tend to be even brighter, and there are innumerable tales of their acting with almost human ingenuity in a wide variety of situations. Their distrust and avoidance of traps and poisoned bait is perhaps not particularly remarkable, since rats are congenitally suspicious of anything new introduced into their terrain, but other frequently-observed aspects of their behaviour are nothing short of astonishing. They have been seen to deliberately dip their tails into partially empty water butts and subsequently suck their appendages, or allow their less agile young to do so, apparently fully aware that to venture right inside would make it difficult for them to get out again via the butt's sloping sides. Certain New Guinea (Trobriand Island) rats go one better and use their tails as fishing lines, dangling them in the sea until they are nipped by crabs, which are then 'reeled in' and consumed. A rather different but equally remarkable example of rat sagacity is recorded by H. Mortimer Batten in his book *British Wild Animals*, wherein he tells of an East Lothian farmer who kept finding a small branch propped up against one of his supposedly rat-proof ricks. The farmer removed the branch each day, but it was unfailingly back in the same position next morning. On the face of it, the conclusion that the rats were deliberately and with foresight using the branch as a bridge seemed inescapable.

If we accept the latter incident at face value – and one has to admit that the evidence for it is somewhat circumstantial – then it is more than probable that those canny Scottish rats worked together to get their ready-made bridge in position, and it is this theme of co-operation that brings us to what is perhaps the most intriguing and controversial of all rat behaviour. That rats actually combine forces to carry away single but otherwise rather unmanageable food items, such as eggs, large potatoes and even fish, to their lairs would seem to be no mere folklore – as many indignant viewers were quick to point out when a recent television programme about rats dismissed the theme as a fable. I myself have notes of literally dozens of such observations, and the significant point is that they vary so little from a common pattern. Essentially what happens, it seems, is that one rat lies on its back, clasping the egg (or whatever) between all four legs and paws, and is then dragged along by the tail, or sometimes the scruff of the neck, by the second; alternatively, the prone rat grasps the leader's tail in its teeth, thus making its passage slightly more comfortable, perhaps, in that it proceeds with the lie of the fur.

Unless we brand all these observers as liars or fancifiers (which in view of their numbers and the wealth of detail commonly offered would be rather insulting), there is no question but that these things happen. What *is* perhaps questionable is our inevitably anthropomorphic interpretation of such behaviour. Sceptical ethologists suggest that it could be explained in terms somewhat removed from deliberate co-operation. They argue, rightly, that a rat is quite capable of abstracting an egg on its own, albeit with some difficulty. Indeed, it contrives to do so by such a variety of observed methods as to suggest that, from this angle alone, rats are very far from being creatures of stereotyped habits but are capable of 'thinking for themselves' to a considerable degree. A rat may grasp an egg to its middle and shuffle along in a sort of sideways motion, or hug it to its chest with its forepaws and hop along on the hind feet like its relative the jerboa or desert rat; alternatively, it bowls the egg along with nose and paws, drags it with looped tail, or even rolls over and over with the item clasped to its belly, rather as stoats have been observed to do. Now, the pragmatic behaviourist goes on to say, what happens when the rat encounters a second rat whilst thus engaged? Quite probably, he says, it will roll over on its back (still clasping the egg), in the submissive attitude typically adopted by individual animals when they happen to meet or clash with others slightly up the social scale. The second, dominant rat then proceeds to rob the robber in the only practical way open to it, dragging both rival and egg back to its lair and there, presumably, laying claim to its prize.

Such an explanation sounds plausible enough, and accords with rats' social behaviour, wherein there is a definite 'pecking order' as to who gets food first, but there are several factors that make it difficult to accept. One has already been mentioned: that it is not infrequently the egg-clasping rat that takes the initiative in the towing business, deliberately hitching a ride, as it were, by grasping the second's tail in its teeth. Another objection is that such co-operative stealings are by no means always simply one-off affairs. Some observers have told of seeing the same pair of rats return several times in order to remove eggs by exactly the same towing method; and there is one truly amazing report from a man who apparently witnessed four rats form a line, one grasping an egg and each holding the tail of the preceding one in its mouth, make off in procession, and then return and repeat the operation until *five* eggs had been abstracted by this elaborate method. The observation is so astounding, not to say incredible, as to make one wonder if an element of fun or play might have been involved in the rats' collective thieving. We are, I have long felt, inclined to under-estimate the possibilities of levity in our fellow animals. That animals *do* play is beyond dispute (see page 61).

Just how one explains such activity other than in obviously anthropomorphic terms it is, therefore, difficult to say. Rats are, as mentioned earlier, highly social animals, and inveterate food-storers, and there seems no reason why they should not be capable of co-operation for the benefit of the community as a whole. In any case, rats also co-operate in other 'human' ways. A New Zealand man tells of a pair that combined to push an awkwardly sized and shaped biscuit through a barred partition, the one tipping it on edge and the other receiving it on the other side, thus achieving their purpose in a way that one rat would have found quite impossible. Helper rats have also been observed to effect the release of fellow rats caught in traps, by gnawing through their tails or legs.

One point worth considering is why rats abstract eggs, and so forth, on their own on some occasions and work co-operatively on others. A significant point here, perhaps, is that 'towing' often seems to occur over uneven or difficult terrain where there would be a greater risk of the prize being broken whilst being bowled or otherwise transported by a single rat. On a number of occasions, two or more rats have been seen working together to remove eggs stored on the shelf of a barn or on a table, the otherwise inevitable smash being avoided through one rat cradling the egg and being deliberately pushed to the ground by the other. Where items of a less frangible nature are concerned, their size and shape might make co-operation useful for that reason alone.

The belief that rats will co-operate to carry away otherwise unmanageable items of food, such as eggs, holds wide currency, as evidenced by this design from a nineteenth-century Japanese fan now in the British Museum's Department of Oriental Antiquities.

So far as I am aware, no fully authenticated photograph of rat co-operative egg-transportation exists. The only one I have seen looks suspiciously like a mock-up or perhaps the photograph of some museum display tableau whose origin has been forgotten. Artistic representations of the theme are, however, commoner and include a superb design on a nineteenth-century Japanese fan, now in the Department of Oriental Antiquities of the British Museum. The illustration accords so closely with reported observations, and is effected with such skill and zoological accuracy, as to make one wonder if the artist had actually witnessed such a happening himself. At any rate, Satake Eikai (1802–74) clearly knew something about rats, even if his information of their curious behaviour was gained only at second-hand. (He might, admittedly, have copied another's drawing.)

In extreme contrast to this, I have a photograph of a combined brass ink- and pounce-pot stand, supposedly nineteenth-century, now in the possession of an Essex clergyman, which seems on the face of it no more than an example of artistic licence run wild, since it shows a rat dragging its prone colleague by the tail, which is slung over the crook of a foreleg and held in the forepaws. What is more, the leader is proceeding forwards, so that it sees where it is going. One might dismiss the concept as an absurd parody of human behaviour, however charming the object is in itself, were it not for the fact that there is a report of a rat duo proceeding along in much this way. In this particular instance, the writer tells of the towing rat holding its fellow's tail over its shoulder, standing on its hind legs and then leaning forward to drag its recumbent partner along in short bursts.

ANIMAL ALTRUISM

Altruism is dictionary-defined as 'helping one's fellows without any thought of personal gain or living for the good of others', and only man is considered capable of it in any conscious sense. I say 'conscious' because it is clear that many animals, especially social groups, *do* work and often sacrifice themselves for the good of the community as a whole. Ants, bees, and mammals like the African dwarf mongoose are prime examples. The difference between human and animal altruism, it is thought, lies in the fact that ours is the result of a deliberate, arbitrary decision, whereas the animal's is pre-programmed, as it were, to come into effect in certain clear-cut ways only. The distinction is not very sharply defined and might even be said to betray a touch of human arrogance; but, by and large, the zoologist argues, when we see animals behaving in what seems a most human-like, unselfish way, they are merely acting instinctively, their altruism being of the genetic kind geared to assist the survival of the *species* and not the individual as such.

Whatever our view of it may be, we need to bear this argument in mind when meeting with instances of animal altruism, however remarkable they seem. There are certainly a great many and some of them again involve rats. I have notes of a number of incidents all purporting to demonstrate that rats, contrary to popular ideas of their nature, show compassion for their old or handicapped, and actually help them in times of need. One of the most interesting of these emanates from a Warwickshire man who tells of a childhood experience when, from the quiet vantage point of a low wall, he watched a trio of rats walking slowly along, side by side, each of them holding the same twig in its mouth. The centre rat, he was intrigued to observe, had only three legs, the two flankers being apparently healthy. In three other similar cases, only one 'helper' was concerned, the led rat being reported as blind; a point that was, in two of the cases, actually proved, since one of the rats was shot and the other found to be quite helpless after its leader had been run over by a car.

One has to admit that, on the face of it, this does indeed look very much like genuine compassionate behaviour, and I would be the last to dismiss such an interpretation out of hand. However, there could be a more pragmatic, less emotionally-charged explanation for it. A rat that had lost a leg would certainly be at a disadvantage and a blind one considerably more so; indeed, it is unlikely that either would survive long thus handicapped. If, however, a blind rat were otherwise healthy it would, while it lived, probably manage to get about fairly well, either by keeping in close contact with its fellows or, more importantly, by following well-defined scent trails, smell being probably the most highly developed of the rat's senses. It would probably not alter its basic behaviour pattern to any marked degree and, in certain circumstances, acting in accordance with its acquisitive nature might instinctively seize anything that a fellow rat happened to be carrying and thus be hauled along, willy-nilly, giving the impression of being led. It is, of course, quite possible that the handicapped rat's instinct for survival also plays some part in such actions, prompting it to grasp items held by another rat intent on returning to its (their) lair. In non-foraging situations, it might even take a colleague's tail in its mouth for this purpose, since such behaviour has actually been observed to occur in rats swimming across rivers in numbers. I am aware of no observation where it was *proved* that the swimming follower was blind or otherwise handicapped, but there seems no reason why it should not happen.

Whether animals do possess glimmerings of true compassion or unselfishness approaching the human kind it is naturally difficult to say, but certain other behavioural examples, involving a variety of species, at least give us pause to think. Whalers have been quick to take advantage of the fact that bottle-nosed whales often appear to show genuine concern for their wounded comrades, which they leave only with apparent reluctance and may actually physically support to prevent their drowning. There are also many instances of apparent altruism in birds. On one occasion a farmer ploughing a field saw part of a furrow fall in and bury one of the crowd of gulls that were following to feed on the exposed insects. The man stopped to rescue the bird but before he reached it he saw one gull pull at the unfortunate's exposed wing-tip and another tug at its head. The farmer completed the rescue but was confident the gull's colleagues would have been capable of performing the task and had every intention of doing so.

Even insects come up with apparent 'helping-out' behaviour. Two American researchers tell of an instance of a cockroach nymph of the African species *Gromphadorhina portentosa* assisting another nymph that is difficult to explain in purely genetic terms. One of the nymphs, it seems, was experiencing difficulty in divesting itself of its exuviae (old cuticle) when the second approached and, after some antennal contact, deliberately peeled off its associate's skin, first from one side and then the other. The observers of this remarkable incident, both of them trained zoologists, stress that the helper nymph made no attempt to eat the finally shed cuticle (something that commonly happens in insects); nor did its action seem to betray some sort of pre-adult courtship behaviour, because neither nymph paid any further attention to each other. No other instance of intra-specific helping was observed in the cockroach group under examination.

Slightly more explicable, perhaps, is the observation of a Chepstow lady who saw a wasp struggling in a spider's web. As she watched, another wasp flew up and tried unsuccessfully to pull its comrade free. It then flew away and returned shortly afterward with two more wasps, all three then pulling and working at the trapped wasp until they finally managed to free it. We might explain such co-operation by suggesting that wasps, and probably most other social insects, emit a distress pheromone (olfactory message) or other signal during times of difficulty, triggering off an automatic reaction and rescue operation from their fellows – but does that really differ so much from, say, a child shouting for help when it is drowning?

Clearly, one has to be careful in weighing up the significance of behaviour like this, more especially where insects are concerned, not least since it can be offset by a somewhat darker, nihilistic side. It is easy to feel that wasps and ants carrying off their wounded, perhaps swatted colleagues are engaged in a sort of ambulance service; unfortunately it is probable that if the injured parties do not recover they will be eaten by their fellows, just as many parent insects (semi-social earwigs, for example) are consumed by their young when they die. In social insects, it seems likely that the individual workers have very little personal identity but function merely as components of the community, geared solely to the rearing of a new generation. If they work well, they are all useful and worth helping for the common good; if they do not, then they are likely to be sacrificed for much the same reason.

Altruism is also known to occur inter-specifically, if naturally much less frequently and usually for rather different reasons. Much of the unselfishness and self-sacrifice shown by dogs toward their human masters probably stems from what the animal behaviourist calls *imprinting*. Taken from its mother at an early age, a pup soon learns to adopt us as its own species, as it were, and develops the protective attitude that goes with it, handed down from its socially organised wild canid ancestors. One can postulate that it is largely this which accounts for the many examples of heroism recorded in dogs, horses and other animals, both in peace and war, when they have often been as steady under fire as their human comrades. To be realistic, one should add that the animals are probably also behaving in a self-interested way when they help their masters. After all, they must surely be aware that to continue to obtain food and shelter they have to do their duty and keep their noses clean.

There are, however, examples of inter-specific helping in other animals which are far more difficult to explain in mechanistic terms, one of them being the apparent friendliness which dolphins show toward human beings, which they are described as actually helping in times of difficulty. Tales of this kind are of extremely ancient origin and form part of the myth and folklore of the Ancient Greeks, Romans, Scandinavians,

Hindus and Polynesians, and other races and civilisations. Herodotus, Cicero, the Plinys (uncle and nephew), Plutarch and Aesop are among classical writers who tell of dolphins saving men and children from drowning by pushing them to the shore or even allowing them to ride on their backs, a motif which the Greeks used on many of their coins. The Greeks also regarded dolphins as sacred – messengers of the gods and symbols of the sea – and in consequence rarely killed them.

That we are not dealing here with mere fables is evidenced by the fact that there are numerous well authenticated accounts of dolphins coming to the aid of man in modern times, in similar ways to those mentioned, as well as towing rowing boats to shore. There is increasing evidence that dolphins actually seem to enjoy the company of people and like to spend time romping and playing with them, especially children. Many explanations have been offered to account for this foible – surely unique among wild animals – but none of them is really convincing, and the dolphin-man relationship still remains one of the world's great animal mysteries. Dolphins have a very large brain, and are undoubtedly intelligent, but one would have thought that this would have made them wary of a species only too ready to kill them for eating too many fish or exploit them as cheap and undignified spectacles.

SYMPATHY AND SORROW

If animals display at least a muted kind of altruism, might they not be equally capable of displaying sympathy or sorrow, perhaps at the loss or illness of one of their own kind? There are many accounts which suggest the possibility of something of the kind, notably in the way various species treat their dead. Rats, grey squirrels, stoats and badgers have all been observed to carry or drag and sometimes actually bury their recently-deceased brethren, occasionally in circumstances remarkably suggestive of sorrow. One naturalist tells of watching a sow badger which appeared at the entrance to her set and began to utter a 'keening' cry, which she kept up for some time until she was joined by a boar. The two then went to ground and reappeared dragging the corpse of a large male. They then combined to drag the body some distance away where they proceeded to inter the corpse, after which the male left the sow by the grave, presenting an irresistible comparison with a human wife wishing to have a few moments alone with her now decently-buried spouse.

Such behaviour is probably unusual although there are records of dead badger cubs being carefully covered with leaves and dry grass and of dead or injured colleagues being hauled off roads, while it is also believed that badgers not infrequently bury their dead in special chambers within the set. (Skulls found in the earth outside badgers' sets

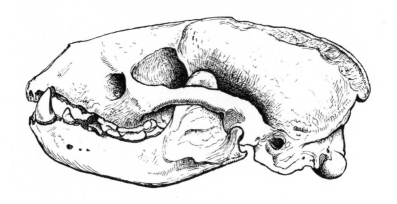

The skull of a badger (**Meles meles**).

would seem to support the contention, although it may of course equally well point to past gassing.) There are, equally, also many tales of swans apparently showing grief over the loss of a mate, lingering near the body and refusing to eat, in precisely the way that one might expect from animals that mate for life. The British politician Jo Grimond tells of a bantam cock which spent a long time ostensibly deeply concerned for a sick hen. The next morning the hen was dead and the cock still in the same position beside her, keening mournfully instead of uttering his usual challenging crow.

Inter-specific sympathy and grief are also by no means unknown, more especially, of course, where domestic animals are concerned. Cats and dogs brought up with each other certainly pine and go off their food if one or other of them dies, and sympathetic behaviour towards their ill or dying master or mistress is also a matter of observed fact. Lest we are moved to think that such apparent regret is as transient as it often is with human relatives, it is only necessary to point to the example of the famous Skye terrier known as 'Greyfriars Bobby', who was so faithful to his master's memory that after following his funeral in 1848 never left the site of his grave until his own death some fourteen years later. The little dog's remarkable fidelity is commemorated in the form of a statue outside the front gate of Greyfriars Church in Edinburgh. However we view such reactions, it is clear that the animals' loss has at least some emotional effect on them, even if we refuse to accept that their sorrow is comparable with man's in similar circumstances and put it all down to self-interest and the loss of a known food-provider.

I have referred elsewhere to the improbability of animals having any very clear idea of right and wrong, since they are basically amoral, as distinct from immoral. This ought, therefore, to dispose of the likelihood of their having any notions of justice or of meting out punishment, as is inherent in the so-called 'rook trials' which have been observed from time to time. In situations of this kind a large group of rooks is seen to surround a single rook, either on the ground or at the top of a tree, after which the supposed miscreant is found or falls to the ground dead. It has been suggested that this is rough justice meted out to inveterate nest (twig) robbers among the rookery residents, but this seems unlikely. More probably the bird was sickly or carrying infection and was thus killed out of collective colony thinking. Such an unsympathetic explanation may seem to run counter to much that has already been described in connection with other animals, yet it too is close enough to much human thinking with regard to hopeless incurables.

The more one explores the intricacies of animal behaviour, and the motives behind it, the more evident it becomes that it differs from man's less in kind than in degree. As we have seen, many species certainly seem to have a sense of fun, even if it is often only an extension of childhood play, which is in itself a practical preparation for adulthood. It is difficult to explain otters' use of special slides into the water other than in these terms, or the observation of a Yardley, Birmingham, man who watched a magpie teasing a fox in his neighbour's garden. The fox was sitting, with its tail stretched right out, when the magpie appeared, walked over and began to repeatedly tweak the fox's brush. The fox did nothing except change its position from time to time, but after about ten minutes appeared to have had enough and jumped the fence into the next garden, urged on its way by the magpie's raucous, chattering cry. Since magpies are unlikely to fall prey to foxes very often, any idea of revenge (even supposing such thoughts possible) seems unlikely as an explanation.

Equally difficult to explain away in purely pragmatic terms is the encounter I once witnessed between a house-fly and a minute spider on my kitchen wall. The spider was simply 'sitting', minding its own business, but the fly seemed bent on mischief. Reversing the usual order of things where spiders and flies are concerned, it kept making little darting runs in the direction of its traditional adversary, always retreating at the last split second to avoid making actual contact. Finally, however, it produced its *pièce de résistance* and boxed the spider's ears, as it were, using its wings to buffet it before instantly flying off. The whole thing was over so quickly that the spider was quite unable to react. I make no attempt to explain the episode, and I rather doubt if anyone could – except, of course, anthropomorphically.

4·ANIMAL WEATHER SIGNS
AND OTHER SENSITIVES

The belief that animals have, in some way, foreknowledge of the weather or of changes in it is probably as old as history itself, although for obvious reasons lore of this kind is most extensive in countries whose climate is uncertain and changeable. In other lands, where the seasonal pattern is more predictable and clear-cut, men had less need to look to the animals for such indications.

Clearly, animals are aware of the passage of the seasons, and act accordingly, so that in this sense, at least, their appearance and activity is linked to climate. In temperate climes, indeed, they are often commonly remarkably consistent in this respect. In Britain, for example, the all black *Bibio marci* is popularly called St Mark's fly, since in average seasons its spring appearance generally coincides with this saint's day (April 25th). The belief that birds mate on St Valentine's Day (February 14th) finds currency throughout much of Europe, and is not entirely fanciful. Similarly, animals make provisions for the advent of harsher, wintry conditions: birds perhaps flying to warmer lands, rodents storing nuts for winter consumption, and insects and other invertebrates going into a state of dormancy before extreme cold actually arrives.

However, all this is unremarkable, since it is linked to animals' ready appreciation of clearly observable and sensible factors: diminishing hours of daylight, increasing warmth or cold, lack of available food, and so on, linked to the pattern of seasonal change. The point is: can animals go further than this and forecast irregularities in the weather to come? Are they, in other words, prescient in the fullest sense of the word? Reluctantly, we have to say 'No', although there are hosts of countrymen and fishing folk who will strongly disagree. Dorset fishermen, for example, are adamant in suggesting that the arrival in January of a large school of porpoises in Christchurch Bay forecasts an early, warm spring. Normally the mammals do not come in close in-shore, principally to calve, until June. Similarly, the spawning of frogs is supposed to provide an indication of the character of the summer to come. Spawn deposited in the middle of a pond allegedly indicates a long, dry summer, that at the edge telling the reverse; all of which is very logical, on the face of it, since the first position would render the egg-mass less liable to desiccation in times of drought, as the pond shrank, whereas that in the latter position would be rendered safe by more frequent rain. The fact is, however, that frog spawn does commonly dry up, and its progenitors seem to take little note of the weather, either at the time it is deposited or later. Frogs and toads not only habitually return to the same waters to breed year after year, whatever their level; they may even breed in what would seem to be strangely adverse conditions, for example when ice is present. The varying position of spawn is probably due to other factors, perhaps the presence or absence of fish or other predators, which might present a greater hazard to frogs, spawn and tadpoles in deeper waters.

Rooks, too, are commonly cited as forecasters of the nature of a summer to come. Beginning their nest-building and egg-laying as early as February, they are said to construct their untidy nests high if the ensuing summer is going to be settled, but much lower if the season is to be changeable, with storms and gales that would have put higher nests at risk. The strange thing about this particular belief is that it should be current among country folk at all, since a little observation of these gregarious nesters would reveal that rooks are great patchers-up and repairers of old nests, which are re-used year after year, until they attain a considerable size and commonly collapse under their own weight. Occupied nests are, in fact, not infrequently blown down by high winds and this can occasionally have an unsettling effect on neighbouring pairs whose nests remain intact, prompting the whole colony to leave *en masse*, perhaps deliberately pulling their nests to pieces before they depart.

Those who cite animals and their behaviour as indicators of *imminent* changes in the weather are on much safer ground, since no-one can doubt that their heightened sensitivity commonly enables them to read the signs far earlier than we can. We may scoff at the widely-held notion that a cat washing behind its ears indicates rain (like many another, no doubt, my mother used to tell our cat not to, more especially just after she had put the washing out!), but readily observed domestic animals, such as cats, dogs and geese, do often seem aware of approaching storms, demonstrating their receptivity of increased static electricity in the atmosphere by heightened activity, vocalisation, and perhaps seeking shelter. A Welsh farmer correspondent of mine told me that he always knew when snow threatened, since his hillside ewes would then make their way into his lambing sheds, whereas in other conditions they were happy to stay out of doors. In much the same vein, a Suffolk man informed me of what seemed, on the face of it, a clear-cut instance of weather-forecasting on the part of his two horses (male and female), kept in a large field. Normally, they would wait until late evening before making their way to the gate for stabling for the night. On this particular occasion, however, they were to be seen standing by the gate at three in the afternoon, and stayed there. Though early winter, conditions were bright and sunny at the time, but then about an hour later the sun was suddenly blotted out by menacing grey clouds, and this was followed by a furious snow-storm together with high winds, all of which seemed to have sprung from nowhere. All the earlier visible signs, my correspondent adds, had seemed to indicate a pleasant, settled day.

Birds are often fairly accurate indicators of what sort of day it is likely to be. A sleepless person lying in bed might well accept an unusually late dawn chorus as an indication of later rain, since birds' song is closely linked to daylight, and overcast skies inhibit such output. The appearance of gulls inland *might* indicate rough weather at sea, as is commonly maintained, except that, in Britain at least, the species most commonly seen scavenging for scraps in fields and on rubbish tips, especially in winter, is the black-headed gull (*Larus ridibundus*), which commonly roosts and nests at large inland lakes and reservoirs and may not have come far. The height at which birds fly is often at least some indication of current and immediately forthcoming weather conditions. Swallows, martins and swifts are among other birds that spend much of their time flying at a considerable height, taking advantage of the airborne 'plankton' of insects drawn upwards by sunlight and the columns of warm air (thermals) rising from the ground. Lower flight could indicate atmospheric changes up aloft which disperse the insects and perhaps bring winds and rain. There is good evidence that swifts have foreknowledge of the imminent arrival of electric storms, since they tend to move out of their path and return after the disturbance has passed.

In some parts of England, notably Buckinghamshire, countrymen point to the strange soaring and tumbling behaviour that carrion crows and rooks indulge in before certain changes in the weather. During this activity, which I have seen myself, the birds fly to a certain height and then let themselves fall, as if shot, repeating the whole business several times. Since 'break-necking', as country people call it, tends to be observed most often in autumn and winter, it is often linked to the imminent advent of rain, snow, sleet and rough winds. It seems probable that the birds actually enjoy being mildly buffeted about by the rapidly changing air currents.

There is some evidence to suggest that animals whose activity is especially closely linked to the weather can be regarded almost as living barometers or even thermometers. Ants typically display heightened activity when the pressure is rising, and swarming in particular tends to be linked with fine settled weather. During this latter activity winged queen and male (drone) ants issue from their nests, accompanied by hosts of excited wingless workers, and climb some eminence before launching themselves into the air, where mating takes place, after which the males die and the females rub off their wings and spend the remainder of their lives establishing new nests and laying eggs. Since ants are poor fliers (and indeed only temporary ones), warm settled conditions aid aerial mating in providing those gentle warm up-currents of air that assist the insects in gaining height. It is even said to be possible to estimate the air temperature to within a few degrees by carefully charting and comparing ants' rate of movement on the ground. Somewhat similar interpretations can, it seems, be made of the way that crickets and grasshoppers vary their rate of chirping according to the ambient temperature. Among several formulae for checking temperature by this esoteric means was that devised by the American physicist A.E. Dolbear who, in 1897, maintained that the thing to do was to count the number of chirps produced in 15 seconds and add 39, the result being an accurate reading to within one or two degrees Fahrenheit. His assessment was apparently geared to the American snowy tree-cricket (*Oecanthus fultoni*) but is said to work with other species, such as the European field-cricket (*Gryllus campestris*).

It seems clear that a great deal of insect weather lore is of this nature, in referring to responses to current conditions, which may or may not be fully apparent to us in the absence of instrumental indication. Certain Carabid or ground-beetles are called 'rain-beetles' in parts of England because they tend to be particularly active on wet evenings which bring worms, their favourite prey, to the surface. They also appear in numbers actually before rain arrives, which doubtless explains why stepping on one was, and perhaps still is, thought to bring on the change. Storm-flies or horse-flies (Tabanidae) may indeed be especially troublesome during hot and humid weather, but it is by no means certain that their heightened activity heralds a storm since it is quite usual for one individual 'host', exuding greater quantities of perspiration and carbon dioxide, to be more prone to attack than another.

Some of the most intriguing supposed animal weather prophets are aquatic. Species of freshwater loaches, notably the so-called 'weatherfish' (*Misgurnus fossilis*) of Europe, apparently gain their group name from the French verb *locher*, to fidget, referring to the restlessness they display when their freshwater home is subjected to barometric, vibratory and temperature influences. Much of this response would seem to be linked to the species' dual adaptation to breathing both water-dissolved and atmospheric air, the latter being especially vital to it when its stream or pond habitat becomes deficient in oxygen or actually dries up. In normal circumstances the fish uses its gills to filter air from the water but in adverse conditions a specially adapted intestinal lung comes into play, enabling the fish to rise to the surface and take gulps of air and expel carbon dioxide from its vent. Such air-breathing is increased as the temperature of the water rises, since the latter then contains less oxygen. The fish is also said to become especially restless some twenty-four hours before a storm, and one explanation for this is said to lie in those structures called Weberian ossicles which link its pressure-sensitive swim-bladder to its inner ear and are especially attuned to interpret minute vibrations. Other fish, such as carp and minnows, possess these structures and also seem at least partially adapted to dual-breathing, which suggests that their responses to atmospheric changes might prove equally revealing.

Freshwater leeches, close relatives of the more familiar earthworm, have been observed to show somewhat similar responses to weather changes, and attempts have been made to patent devices involving them as living barometers and storm indicators. A Victorian encyclopaedia entitled *Enquire Within* tells us, for example, that a leech kept in a large jar will lie motionless at the bottom during fine, settled weather, but if rain, snow or some other such change is due creeps to the very top and stays there until conditions are more settled. Should storms or high winds be on the way, we are told, the leech moves 'through its habitation with amazing swiftness, and seldom goes to rest until it begins to blow hard.' The celebrated Great Exhibition, held at London's Crystal Palace in 1851, displayed a leech storm-glass, in which leeches would ring a tiny

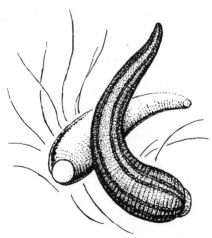

Medicinal leeches (***Hirudo medicinalis***). Their variable movements have been taken to indicate changes in the weather. Slightly enlarged.

bell when they rose to the surface to warn of an approaching tempest. Its ingenious inventor, the appositely named Dr Merryweather, also drew up a chart indicating the positions the leeches assumed during forecasted sunshine, rain and storm. Unfortunately their lordships of the Admiralty rejected the good doctor's suggestion that they should adopt such instruments to aid them in predicting coastal storms. They were probably wise to do so since while one cannot doubt that leeches and many other animals are sensitive to changes in barometric pressure, and show it in their behaviour, they are equally not robots and other influences may affect their movements. Dr Merryweather seems to have used the then far commoner medicinal leech (*Hirudo medicinalis*) for his device, which could lead to all sorts of problems, notably in that human proximity (more particularly, body heat) might induce the leeches to try to leave the water and make straight for such promising sources of nourishment. In my experience, a tank containing a number of such leeches will generally reveal one or two of them out of the water, climbing up the sides, apparently intent on self-destruction through desiccation, with others swimming about or resting on the bottom. Such variable behaviour clearly renders leeches rather difficult to assess as accurate weather-forecasters.

EXTRA SENSES

Animals' heightened sensitivity manifests itself in a variety of ways that look like genuine prescience. Instances of zoo animals becoming unusually restless and disturbed just prior to the advent of destruction-bringing forces like earthquakes, avalanches and erupting volcanoes are, for example, well documented. In Japan, where earthquakes are almost a way of life, goldfish (members of the carp family, whose receptivity has already been postulated) have long been accepted as near infallible prophets of these disturbances, warning of their approach by exhibiting almost frantic movements through the water, which forms an excellent conductor of sounds and seismic vibrations.

Animals may also, it seems, warn man against the depredations of his own kind, a well-known, if somewhat apocryphal, example being the sacred geese on the Roman Capitoline Hill which, according to Plutarch, alerted citizens to imminent atack by the barbarian Gauls in 390 BC by setting up a constant, excited cackling. Another tells of those house-nesting storks which abandoned their homes just before the Adriatic town of Aquileia was sacked by Attila the Hun in 476. Among modern parallels may be mentioned the duck which, in 1944, began quacking loudly and persistently just before an Allied air-raid over Freiburg, in Germany. Despite the fact that the sirens had failed to sound, many citizens accepted the bird's unwonted excitement as a genuine warning, took to the shelters, and were consequently saved. In recognition of the duck's unwitting services, a statue of it was erected to commemorate the event. There are, in addition, reports of cats and other animals reacting agitatedly to the advent of bombers approaching British cities and towns during World War 2, long before the human inhabitants were aware of the threat.

If cases like these can probably be explained merely in terms of a five-sensory perception infinitely superior to our own, others are considerably more baffling. Not long ago a retired farmer wrote to tell me of a foal which always heralded the return of its mother from market by becoming wildly excited about half an hour before she actually arrived, neighing loudly and drumming its hooves against the door of its stable. Since the mare's return times were otherwise unpredictable, the farmer's family used the foal's reactions as a cue for putting the kettle on for the returning marketeers' tea! Just what subtle signals the foal was receiving from its still far-distant mother it is difficult, if not impossible, to say. It seems hardly likely that supersensitivity of smell or hearing played a part in the animal's reactions, at such a distance and in view of its enclosed situation, which only leaves some extra sense, beyond the accepted five. Was it telepathy?

Clearly, animals employ a whole range of visual, auditory and chemical signals for communication purposes, many of which are beyond our interpretation without mechanical means, and we cannot deny the possibility of mind or thought waves coming into play as well, more particularly perhaps in circumstances where intense emotions are concerned. They may even operate between beast and man, if usually only in the one direction. My father swears that when ploughing with his pair of heavy horses – one a shire, the other a dappled grey percheron – they would sense if he were irritated or had something on his mind and prove uncooperative. One lady tells of her dog which reacted to her apparently purely mental decision to take him to the veterinary surgeon, to have his injured paw re-treated, by hiding under the bed. The problem with episodes like this is that we cannot be sure whether the animals were responding to subtle behavioural signals rather than thought-waves.

There are several alleged instances of animals communicating with man on a two-way, purely mental level, both understanding and being understood, but they are rare and difficult to confirm. The plain fact is that man is not really equipped for such things. He will undoubtedly continue to make progress in his understanding of animals at a purely physical level but because his senses (and extra senses) are dull by comparison, a deeper comprehension of them, their motives and ways of thinking, is likely to elude him. Even with the most supremely intelligent animals, such as dolphins, whose brains are larger even than ours, closer contact and comprehension will probably founder on a human lack of sensitivity – using the word in its widest meaning or 'sense'. It is surely no accident that very young children are often more fully accepted by animals than adults, since the junior mind is less burdened with matter-of-fact knowledge and concerns which, in maturity, tend to push 'finer feelings' and almost everything else out of the way.

Perhaps the main obstacle in the way of our understanding animal 'thinking' lies in the natural wariness with which nearly all species regard *Homo sapiens*. Man, after all, is the only animal to slaughter other species without good reason. Based on the arrogant assumption that he is the 'master' and the only truly reasoning species on Earth, he has no compunction about killing or exploiting other animals as and when it suits him. As a result, most animal species are careful (and wise) to give man a very wide berth. Only rarely do they come halfway to meet him, as it were on a spiritual level, and then, again, it is usually only during moments of intense emotion. In his book *The Psychic Power of Animals*, Bill Schul tells of a man who was deliberately approached by a lynx whilst walking in a forest, normally something that would be quite unheard of, since lynxes are exceedingly shy of man, rarely seen, as well as being both fierce and powerful. On this occasion, however, both lynx and man overcame their basic mistrust of one another, the man holding his ground until the big cat stopped in front of him and looked at him with what seemed mingled pain and appeal in its eyes. Then the man saw that the lynx's mouth was grossly swollen through one of its teeth having pierced its tongue. Displaying unusual courage and confidence, he gently worked the tongue free, an operation which took several minutes and must have caused the lynx considerable pain. The latter, however, underwent the operation without complaint, looked at the man with glowing eyes after it was over, and then murmured a soft 'mrrroww' before slipping away silently into the woods. Such heart-warming happenings make the legend of Androcles and the lion seem considerably more plausible.

5·FEARS AND PHOBIAS

SNAKES: MALIGNANT OR MALIGNED?

To say that snakes are just about the least liked of all the animals would be putting it mildly. Opinion polls, conducted with both adults and children, consistently place these fascinating reptiles at the very bottom of any Animal Popularity League, although the reasons for such anathema are tenuous to say the least, since it is apparent in countries where there are few, if any, venomous species at all. Something of this basic antipathy can perhaps be linked to the age-old designation of the serpent as the personification of evil, not merely in the Biblical creation story but in many other religious creeds. However, it probably goes deeper than that and may well be the heritage of some half-forgotten race memory shared, it seems, by our closest evolutionary relatives, the apes and monkeys. Zoologist Dr Desmond Morris has demonstrated that a chimpanzee, for example, will treat even a toy snake with the deepest suspicion, even when having lived all its life in captivity with no opportunity of seeing a living specimen. Many people, especially women, react in precisely the same way. Can the instinctive fear, one wonders, be traced back to remote times when men and woman (perhaps carrying babies) were more vulnerable, shorter-lived and, of course, lacked any form of effective treatment? The curious thing is that today's very young children commonly display no fear of snakes whatsoever and it has been shown that only after the age of about four or five does the distrust begin to manifest itself, whether as a result of increasing awareness or parental influence it is difficult to say.

What *is* certain is that snakes are grossly maligned. Of the 2700 or so known species, only about 400 have venom glands at all and, while some are undoubtedly more irascible than others, it is doubtful if any attacks man on sight without prior provocation. When bites do occur, it is nearly always because deliberate handling or interference has taken place or there has been trespass on the reptiles' breeding territory. Logic confirms the basic argument, since snakes use their venom for two purposes only:

to overcome their prey and for defence. Since no venomous species exceeds a length of some 16–18 feet (5–5.5 m), and has a modest girth to match, the deliberate expenditure of toxin on man would be a useless exercise, so far as any addition to its diet were concerned. Snakes can only swallow their prey whole; they cannot chew or bite pieces off.

Nevertheless, tales of snake aggressiveness continue to proliferate, both in fiction and purported fact. Old sweats eagerly relate the perils undergone from having deadly Indian kraits (*Bungarus* spp.) deliberately drop onto the head from trees and awnings, while the intrepid explorer is regularly put to flight by droves of snakes which chase him to the point of exhaustion. Neither is true. Nor is a pregnant woman likely to have her milk tainted by a snake's venom, should she have the misfortune to be bitten, although such notions are still widely held.

Even in countries like Britain, which supports only one venomous snake, the retiring adder or viper (*Vipera berus*), popular antipathy is rife and campaigns of slaughter continue apace. One might have thought that reason would come into the matter rather more today but sadly this is by no means always the case and support for adder destruction comes from the most reprehensible quarters. Only recently, a certain Member of Parliament suggested that the adder should be systematically exterminated as a British species because he had come across some in his garden and one had bitten his dog. By the same token, one might argue, with infinitely greater justification, that all motorised vehicles be banned because people are injured and killed by them. In fact, fatalities from adder bites are so rare as to hardly merit assessment. All known records in Britain indicate that they barely extend into double figures, and it is probable that the death-rate is scarcely higher in Europe, where there are admittedly one or two more venomous species, such as the asp viper (*Vipera aspis*) and the little sand boa (*Eryx jaculus*) of the Balkans. Most of the real problems with snake bites tend to occur in warmer, especially tropical countries, which combine a large number of poisonous species with exacerbating problems of malnutrition and inefficient treatment, plus a tendency on the part of locals to walk barefoot or inadequately shod. Countries like India and Burma consistently display the highest number of snake-bite casualties every year for precisely these reasons.

Similar semi-hysterical sensationalism tends to be applied to the large constricting snakes, the pythons and anaconda. People *have* been killed and eaten by them, but it is very far from being a common experience. Most adult humans are too large, bulky and active to be swallowed, although those in any doubt whilst confronting one might care to bear it in mind that a python or anaconda does *not* need to anchor its tail in order to overcome its victim. Nor does a constricting snake crush its prey to death. Such snakes use their powerful coils to restrict a seized animal's breathing, each time the victim gulps for breath tightening their hold still further, so that the prey is literally suffocated.

Exaggerations of size present another aspect of snake lore that tends to heighten their terror-inspiring effect. Distortions of this kind are most spectacularly applied to the great constrictors, though all snakes can be assured of having their length and thickness almost doubled by the eye of faith. In his fascinating book *Dangerous to Man*, Robert Caras tells of a traveller who described a South American anaconda with a head 3 feet (1 m) wide, eyes like tennis balls, and an overall length of 140 feet (43 m)! The sober fact is that while *Eunectes murinus* is the largest known snake, there are no properly authenticated records of it ever exceeding a length of about 40 feet (12 m), and even such 'monsters' as this are happiest when confining their dietary attentions to small, more easily digested mammals. Clearly, there is something built in to man's psychological make-up – some sort of defence mechanism, perhaps – that automatically brings an element of magnification into play where unpleasing creatures are concerned.

RATS IN REALITY

For many people, rats, not snakes, are the ultimate horror. Widely regarded as dirty, disease-ridden and cowardly, yet ever ready to attack in numbers, they are inextricably associated in the popular imagination with evil-smelling sewers and dungeons – an image heightened by their frequent portrayal in this light in 'Gothic' horror stories, wherein our hero is confined with and constantly threatened by them. Often, in case we do not have the message, there is a heap of well-gnawed skeletons close by, suggesting that this will be *his* fate unless he can escape.

The fact is that this lurid picture of rats' ways is almost complete fiction: a gross aspersion on their character. First of all, rats are exceedingly clean creatures, almost obsessed with personal hygiene. They spend hours grooming themselves from head to toe and, like monkeys and apes, will even groom each other, though that, admittedly, is more for social bonding purposes than anything else. They certainly like sewers and other smelly places but that is only because, being scavengers, they can find excellent food pickings there. They are certainly no more cowardly (or brave) than any other animal.

It would, of course, be wrong to imply that rats do not occasionally bite people, but closer analysis of reported instances tends to show that such 'aggressiveness' almost invariably occurs only when the rats are injured or cornered. In other words, they react out of pain or plain fright, their first instinct being to run away. A rat will certainly try to bite if struck at with a stick or, as sometimes happens, if driven up the nearest human leg after being chased by a terrier. But, then, who can blame it? Indeed, I have often wondered just how it is that those who kill and harass animals profess to be so shocked and amazed when their intended victims actually have the temerity to try to defend themselves.

Even within a confined space, rats do not make a habit of attacking man, whether in numbers or otherwise. Highly intelligent and nervous creatures, they are intensely suspicious of anything strange and untried, especially if it is large and obviously living. Thus an active man who leaves rats strictly alone whilst in their company has really very little to fear from them. Even if he were tied up, and the rats starving and unable to escape, they would probably do no more than give him a few exploratory sniffs, preferring to cannibalise their own smaller and weaker brethren before paying him any closer, more sinister attention. Ultimately, they might perhaps nibble his exposed extremities – ears, nose, toes, fingers – but they would be most unlikely to eat him alive, though if he died he would not be wasted: they would undoubtedly consume his corpse, bones and all. It may be significant to mention here that tame rats amplify the view of wild rats being far less aggressive than is popularly supposed, since they are much less inclined to bite the handler than mice or even the highly popular hamsters and guinea-pigs. (Fiction does not always get the rat image wrong, incidentally. Edgar Allan Poe's short story 'The Pit and the Pendulum' is among those very few literary offerings that really do the animal justice.)

One rat characteristic that tends to increase suspicion of it in the popular eye is its communal living, more especially those occasional mass movements made when a newly-matured generation of young rats is forcibly expelled from the home terrain by the older incumbents. These migrations are not frequently seen, since they normally take place at night, but to anyone brought up on a diet of rat horror must present a daunting sight when they are occasionally observed during the daytime. My father tells of seeing just such a rat exodus crossing a lonely minor road along which he was cycling. Relating that they took some time to pass into the neighbouring field, accompanying their jostling progress with much excited squeaking, and freely admitting to sharing the near-universal belief that rats will unhesitatingly swarm all over anyone who crosses their path, my father was content to watch from a safe distance, and only proceeded on his way after he was quite certain they had all gone.

Mention has been made elsewhere of the tendency to exaggerate the size of less popular animals, and rats have not escaped such further distortion of their fearsome image. There is, apparently, one reliable record of a brown rat weighing nearly 3½ lb (1.5 kg), but that is by way of being an exceedingly rare exception. Most weigh 7–12 ounces

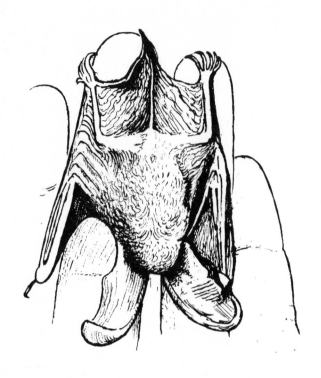

This long-eared bat (***Plecotus auritus***), clinging to the author's hand, died soon after the drawing of it was made and had probably suffered some injury.

(200–340 g), with a body length of about 7 inches (18 cm) and a tail an inch or so shorter. Black rats (*Rattus rattus*) tend to be smaller, slighter and less heavy, though with a proportionately longer tail. The so-called giant rats (*Cricetomys*) of Africa, and somewhat similar genera occurring in New Guinea, are indeed relative giants, attaining a length of 3 feet (90 cm); however, they scarcely fit the popular rat image, being solitary and herbivorous, as well as retiring and inoffensive in the extreme. Incidentally, the legendary/fictional king (that is, giant) rat has no connection with the so-called 'rat kings', apart from the fact that rats are involved. The latter present a unique and inexplicable phenomenon, consisting as they do of groups of perhaps 6–12 rats (usually *Rattus rattus*), whose tail-tips have become inextricably entangled. Most 'kings' have been reported from Europe and Asia, the earliest in 1564, with others turning up as recently as 1963. So far, no-one has been able to suggest a really convincing explanation of how or why the rats get themselves into such a mess.

BATS

To the mediaeval man-in-the-street, steeped as he was in a firm belief in witches and warlocks and the 'black arts' in general, bats must have seemed like indisputable minions of the devil. After all, what else could one think of creatures that not only chose to flit about in pitch darkness but did so in complete and utter silence and, moreover, were such obvious *hybrids*, with the body and features of a particularly fiendish-looking mouse and the membraneous wings one associated principally with dragons? Thus it was that Satan himself was commonly depicted as having bat wings, and any poor lonely old woman who had a colony of bats roosting in or near her dwelling was liable to be branded a witch, especially if she happened to be a little 'odd' in other ways.

Later opinion tended to tone down such extreme attitudes into one that regarded the bat as simply unlucky, although the more sinister implications were a long time dying. A bat that flew three times around one's house was a sure sign of imminent death; one actually entering it guaranteed a whole string of disasters; while a bat flying close by you was still half suspected of having come straight from that old woman, who was quite possibly trying to bewitch you.

It would doubtless be hard to find anyone owning to such strange fancies today, yet it is not unlikely that they have filtered down to contribute to the rather more muted prejudice with which these little winged mammals are currently regarded by womenfolk, in particular. Ladies are typically uneasy about the proximity of bats because they believe, or have been influenced into believing, that there is a constant danger of them flying into and entangling themselves in their hair, presumably based, at least partly, on the erroneous concept of bats as being blind and their flight consequently a rather hit-and-miss affair.

On the face of it, the whole idea sounds quite absurd, especially when we investigate bats' nocturnal navigation and other activity rather more closely. First of all, bats are very far from being blind: their eyes are both moderately large and perfectly developed, if undesigned for nocturnal vision. In any case, the point is largely irrelevant, since bats employ a quite different sense while flying in total darkness: an exceedingly efficient system of echo-location, analogous to our own radar and sonar. From the mouth or, in the case of the curious horseshoe bats, the nose, they emit a stream of ultrasonic pulses which bounce off obstacles or insect prey and are received again by the bat, which is thus able to gauge both their position and distance at lightning speed. So effective is their radar that the possibility of bats making an error of judgement or colliding with something in their path is reduced to a minimum. Bats released in a room which has been criss-crossed with numerous exceedingly fine threads evade contact with them in each and every case.

Having said that, bats' radar is not quite infallible. Perhaps because of inexperience or some injury to the ear, nose or wing, accidents do occasionally occur. Bats have been known to collide with walls and entangle themselves in netting or wire mesh, and there have been observations of Daubenton's or water bats (*Myotis daubentoni*) striking anglers' night-lines, apparently misled by the movements of float and the ripples caused by it into taking them for insect prey, which species like this commonly catch when swooping low over the water. Possibly something of the kind forms the basis of the bat-in-the-hair belief, since it would take only a few accidental contacts with the person to establish it in that shadowy world of half-fact, half-fiction of which legends are made.

There are, in fact, a number of published reports of bat collisions with people in the natural history literature. In one of them, E. Kay Robinson, founder of the British Naturalists' Association and its official journal *Country-Side*, echoed women's fears by stressing how difficult he had found it to free a bat once it entangled itself in the female tresses by its claws, which are present not merely on the feet but on the leading margins of the wings. Two lady 'victims' whom I was actually able to catechise about their experiences made much the same point: one telling of having to physically pull the bat free, the other reporting that the bat had actually bitten or scratched her on the cheek *en passant*. An interesting aspect of these incidents is that both occurred whilst the women were proceeding – one walking, the other cycling – down a tree-bordered road, illuminated by street lamps, since this suggests another possible reason for collisions. Bats typically use such terrains to hawk back and forth for insect food, which they periodically take to the trees to consume at leisure in their characteristic upside-down position. Very much creatures of habit, they soon learn to accommodate to illumination and may even actually switch off their echo-location mechanism in such situations, relying principally on vision; and it is in circumstances like this that visual dazzle, perhaps leading to accidental impact with people or other obstacles, might occur. It is certainly known that bats navigate by sight in permanently lit situations, for example in public-visited cave systems, and the effects of dazzle have also been observed, one man telling, a few years ago, of seeing a bat fly across a road and become so bemused by the glare of the adjacent street lamp as to crash into the telegraph wires above it. Anyone passing by a street lamp or displaying a bicycle headlight at the precise instant that a bat was flying over might suffer 'attack' from this cause.

There is one further possible explanation. It has been suggested that occasional human contact might occur in the rather unlikely eventuality of young bats falling from their parent's body onto human heads below. Such things are scarcely feasible out of doors but might have occurred

Vampire bats (***Desmodontidae***) are confined to Central and South America.

with greater frequency in times past when bats commonly roosted and bred in old-fashioned ceiling-less houses.

One must emphasise that the likelihood of having a bat collide with or entangle itself in the hair is not great; it could even be said to be extremely remote. Bats are not the slightest bit interested in us, except as things to be avoided, and this they generally do with consummate ease. After all, they have had plenty of time to practise. Palaeontological evidence indicates that they and their built-in radar system have been around for 50,000,000 years, which rather tends to put man and his own fifty-year use of echo-location techniques in the shade!

One aspect of bat lore that *does* belong almost solely to the realm of pure fancy concerns vampires. Slavonic in origin, the vampire of folklore and fiction is essentially 'human' and any link with bats is wholly imaginative. Vampire bats do exist but they are exclusively Neotropical in distribution, being confined to Central and South America. The bats clearly derive their epithet from the two-legged, bat-winged blood-drinkers, and not the other way about, since they can only have become at all familiar to Europeans subsequent to the pioneering explorations of the sixteenth-century Spanish and Portuguese, and tales of Dracula-type vampires are considerably older than that. In any case, vampire bats do *not* suck blood: they make an incision with their sharp teeth and lap up the blood that wells out as a result, dribbling some of their saliva into the wound to prevent coagulation. They occasionally attack humans, especially if protective mist-nets are not used, but more usually confine their attentions to deer and domestic animals. Only a few ounces of blood are taken at a sitting but because of a tendency to transmit diseases, such as rabies, their attentions can be both unwelcome and dangerous. All other bat species are either insectivorous or fruit-eaters and are, in consequence, innocuous to man.

ARACHNOPHOBIA

Arachnophobia, the morbid fear of spiders, is shared by countless numbers of people throughout the world and is apparently as ineradicable as it is irrational. It is quite useless for the arachnologist to protest that of the 30,000 or so known species only about half a dozen possess anything approaching lethal bites, that the majority are so small as to be unable even to pierce the skin, and that none of them is intent on running up the nearest leg or dropping down (deliberately) onto the head. All falls on deaf ears. Indeed, it is clear that arachnophobes are less concerned about spiders' ability to bite than their appearance and habits. The possession of eight (often long) legs, hairy bodies, and scuttling movements, frequently conducted in darkness or inaccessible corners, awakens some primitive, perhaps innate, horror and repulsion that no amount of logical argument can ever hope to overcome. The anonymous writer of the Scottish prayer requesting the Good Lord to deliver us from 'long-leggety beasties' during the night surely had spiders principally in mind! For many, spiders are no more than Hieronymous Bosch's pictures of goblins and devils come to life.

Many European countries are without even one species of spider whose bite is in any way dangerous, even supposing the latter were suffered in the first place (which would only be the result of rough handling); yet arachnophobia is as deeply engrained and widespread there as anywhere in the world, perhaps more so. The mere sight of some long-legged house spider scampering across the living room carpet or marooned in the bath is enough to send ladies, in particular, into near hysterics, although such reactions are not entirely confined to the fair sex. Cardinal Wolsey is said to have found Hampton Court Palace quite uninhabitable because of its healthy population of 'Cardinal' spiders (*Tegenaria parietina*). One notable latter-day arachnophobe is the British journalist Bernard Levin, who admits to feeling quite ill at the mere sight of *any* spider, whatever its size.

The curious thing is that such attitudes do not invariably extend to the phobic's wishing to kill the object of his or her loathing. In Scotland, for example, it is considered extremely unlucky to kill one: a heritage, perhaps, of the inspiration to persevere that Robert the Bruce (1274–1329) is said to have gained from watching a spider repair its web. All most spider-haters desire, it seems, is for the creature to be taken out of their way. Many cannot even bring themselves to touch a dead spider and have been known to see spiders where there is none – in a feather or the discarded calyx of a tomato, for example. Ironically, such extreme attitudes may in themselves bring certain dangers, not from the spider itself but as a result of the phobic's frantic efforts to avoid contact with it. One lady, having found a large spider in her bath, carried it downstairs in a duster with the object of freeing it outside. Halfway down, the spider escaped and ran down her blouse, causing the woman to panic, lose her balance and fall downstairs, breaking her leg. Drivers have been known to lose control of their vehicles and become involved in serious accidents through brushing spiders off their body.

As already mentioned, dangerous spiders are few and certainly not aggressive so far as man is concerned. Most are confined to warm climates, although some tend to take up residence in houses or other buildings, which increases the chances of being bitten and scarcely helps the spiders' image in general. A notable example is the famous southern black widow (*Latrodectus mactans*) which occurs mainly in the southern parts of the USA, down to South America and islands beyond. The female's bite is far more toxic than the male's and can be exceedingly unpleasant, its nerve-venom being said to be fifteen times more potent than that of a rattlesnake. Fortunately, only a very small amount of venom is injected, so that even before the widespread use of antitoxin fatalities tended to be few and restricted to children or the old and frail. The black widow is said to have a particular liking for outdoor toilets, with occasional consequences that are probably best left to the imagination! Related species of *Latrodectus* occur in Australia, the Pacific and Africa, while the Australians also have to contend with the Sydney funnel-web spider (*Atrax robustus*), another frequent commensal of man, with an extremely potent bite which led to severe symptoms before the recent development of an antivenin especially designed to deal with it.

One of the curiosities of spider venom is that its toxicity seems quite unrelated to its possessor's size. All of the species so far mentioned are relatively small yet with toxins that can, in extreme circumstances, cause death. By contrast, the very largest species, the Mygalomorphs or bird-eating spiders of the Americas, produce bites which are no more serious and painful than a bee-sting. In fact, it is likely that the greatest risk from handling one of these great spiders lies in their tendency to readily shed the irritant hairs that cover their abdomen. It is, in truth, only their size that renders these spiders so suitable as horror elements in films, since they are far from dangerous and, indeed, are frequently sold as pets.

Mygalomorph spiders are popularly referred to as 'tarantulas', but this is really a misnomer. The true tarantula is a very much smaller wolf-spider (*Lycosa narbonensis*), a native of southern Europe. Its bite is reported to be toxic enough to kill small mammals and birds, and is also said, on somewhat dubious authority, to have been responsible for those outbreaks of hysterical dancing, or tarantism, which occurred in parts of Italy during the fifteenth to seventeenth centuries and still occasionally manifests itself today, notably in the Apulia region. The species gains its name from the city of Taranto, where such continuous dancing was apparently advocated as a cure for the spiders' bites – the wild movements being considered efficacious in sweating out and dispersing the venom. (The tarantella dance is said to derive from the same manic source.)

Just what caused (or causes) tarantism is a mystery. Clearly it had something more than spider-bites behind it, since it is extremely unlikely that such a retiring, ground-living species as *Lycosa narbonensis* would be responsible for more than the very occasional bite. Whether it was purely psychological or the manifestation of heightened religio-superstition, admixed with a good measure of arachnophobia thrown in, we simply cannot say.

'CREEPY-CRAWLIES'

Non-naturalists employ 'creepy-crawly' as a term of semi-opprobrium for a whole range of invertebrates that creep, crawl or even fly. Whether they are active by day or night, or can bite or sting, scarcely matters: it is their 'alien' appearance and habits that causes them to be regarded with suspicion and even horror. It is an attitude that popular newspapers, in particular, seem to delight in intensifying. Any large exotic insect with the misfortune to be imported in a cargo of fruit is liable to find itself seized upon (metaphorically, of course!) and the readers' blood chilled with blown-up photographs of it, together with captions that proclaim it as the 'beastie', 'thingy' or even 'alien invader'. Finders and eye-witnesses of the discovery seem equally pre-programmed to utter the expected comments indicative of extreme horror and loathing. Needless to say, the insects or whatever are almost invariably totally harmless, although of course it would never do to say so. Such things help to fill editorial space and sell newspapers.

Entomologists might be inclined to regard such sensationalism as a joke, and leave it at that, were it not for the fact that people tend to believe what they read in the popular press and disregard the advice of those truly in the know. Nor are 'spokesmen' and 'experts' entirely blameless in the matter, since they, too, are equally responsible for a lot of misapprehensions about insects and other invertebrates. A year or two ago, for example, a cargo of crickets, destined as food for pet chameleons, escaped from their containers whilst being transported by train, causing near panic among the passengers, one or two of whom were, it seems, bitten. The experts subsequently consulted blithely affirmed that the crickets were indeed 'capable of mounting a modest assault on humans': a statement conducive to misunderstanding, to say the least. Crickets can certainly bite and are, indeed, carnivorous, but they prefer other insects to man, and to suggest that the crickets would actually gang up with people as their object, however 'modest' their assault, is the height of irresponsibility. I have not investigated the circumstances of those bites that are alleged to have occurred, but I doubt if there were many, and they would certainly not have been serious.

Government departments and industry are also commonly responsible for increasing people's already deep-seated suspicion of the insect tribe as a whole. A recent advertisement from Britain's Energy Efficiency Office incorporated a composite illustration of some 70 insects and invertebrates which were supposed to make their creepy way into uninsulated cavity walls. They included glow-worm, Buprestid beetle, lobster moth caterpillar and a whole host of other species which the entomologist would be glad to come across in free nature, never mind in such ridiculously impossible situations as the one suggested.

Needless to say, those insects that bite or sting have come in for a particularly large number of broadsides, especially from the pharmaceutical industry. One such company, advertising an anthisan cream for the treatment of stings, illustrated bumble and carder bees as regular stingers of people, and the hornet as dangerous and aggressive. The fact is that the Bombidae are so mildly disposed as to be handled with impunity, while the hornet (*Vespa crabro*) is far less aggressive than the average wasp and in Britain, at least, has become increasingly rare. To 'stir up a hornets' nest' is an expression which shows just how far the average insect-hater is divorced from reality, since there are records of nests being damaged with no consequent reaction from the occupants. The author has even allowed a hornet to crawl over his hands without suffering the consequences that public opinion insists would ensue.

Of course, people *do* get stung and since only the Hymenoptera possess proper stings (actually modified ovipositors or egg-laying tools), it is principally the bees, wasps, hornets and ants that are the culprits. Of these, by far the most aggressive (we should really say defensively aggressive) are the ants, as anyone who has sat on the ground near a red ants' nest will know. Red ants (*Myrmica* sp.) are very small but their sting can be intensely painful, fully as bad as the most virulent nettles, and quite disproportionate to their size. Those who live in the tropics, as well as America and Australia, have things even worse. The fire ant (*Solenopsis saevissima*) of the USA has a particularly agonising sting, while the inch-long bulldog ants (*Myrmecia* sp.) of Australia, armed with both powerful stings and huge, serrated-edged jaws, have been known to make picnickers take to their heels. Most ants sting simply because humans happen to be in their way, but there are a few which can be regarded as genuinely aggressive. These so-called driver- and army-ants of Central and South America, Africa and India are virtually unstoppable once they are on the move in search of food for a new generation of larvae, and any animal, however large, that could not get out of the way would undoubtedly be in peril of its life from a combination of multiple stings and bites. Tales of these ants killing and eating horses, cattle and even, occasionally, people may well be true, since ants like these are true carnivores, their spectacular movements and appetites being directly linked to the sheer enormity of their populations, which can literally run into millions.

Actually, a number of ant species cannot sting, although it may sometimes seem that they can. The little black ants (*Lasius niger*) of Europe that commonly invade houses in summer to scavenge on food scraps may irritate if they happen to get on the skin but this is due merely to the drops of formic acid which the ants dribble from their modified poison glands, the effect being infinitely less painful than when actually injected. Only those displaying allergic reaction are likely to suffer anything more than a mild itching from such causes. Wood ants (*Formica rufa*) are equally stingless, but make up for the disability by being able to squirt acid upward for several inches, generally when gathered for defence at the tops of their nest mounds.

Despite popularly expressed views to the contrary, hive or honey bees (*Apis mellifera*) are scarcely more aggressively inclined than bumbles (*Bombidae*), unless one happens to be a direct line with their foraging route. (I have known cricketers and bowls players suffer in this respect!) Queens appear to have a steadying influence on colonies, as those eccentrics taking part in 'bee-beard' competitions at an American university can attest. The queens are here attached to the competitors' chins enclosed in a small container and the workers attracted to them cluster in their thousands about the contestants' face and chest. The latter are, it seems, rarely if ever stung. Having said that, there seems little doubt that honey bees are inclined to be temperamental. The Roman poet Virgil is said to have secreted his valuables in the middle of his beehives, and it was probably one of the safest places in the circumstances, since uninitiates approaching hives may not invariably get away unscathed. Had the author of the *Aeneid* and the *Georgics* been able to use the giant Indian honey-bee (*Apis dorsata*) or the African race of the hive bee (*Apis mellifera adansonii*) his property might have been even safer, since both are considerably more intolerant of intruders on their territory and have been known to put large animals, like jaguars, to flight.

One difference between the stings of honey bees and wasps, apart from the chemical nature of their venom, lies in the fact that those of the former cannot generally be withdrawn, whereas bumble bees, wasps, hornets and ants can sting repeatedly with impunity. Since Apis stings are barbed, they tend to lodge in the skin of mammalian attackers, in particular, and cannot be retracted without disembowelling the stinger.

On the face of it, this ought to suggest that wasps would be the more belligerent of the two, but this is not so. Most wasp stings occur when the insects are trapped in the clothing or repeatedly swatted at. Tales of 'swarms' of wasps actually chasing people, perhaps after nest disturbance, are arrant nonsense. Wasps simply do not behave in that way or even swarm about a queen as honey bees do. Some tropical vespids have particularly painful stings but generally the only real danger to man from

Many insects, like this wasp-beetle (*Clytus arietis*), imitate the coloration and even behaviour of their wasp 'models', but are quite harmless. Slightly enlarged.

either wasps or bees comes in the rare event of multiple stings or if the victim happens to be stung in the mouth or throat, which could cause swelling and choking.

While most insects will try to bite if restrained in the hand (that is, if they have biting mouthparts in the first place, which not all do), and some beetles, in particular, can discharge irritant substances, they are rarely a hazard simply because deliberately handling them is the very last thing that occurs to most people. Children tend to be more adventurous in this respect and, together with inexperienced entomologists, have been known to suffer severe skin rashes from handling the caterpillars of certain moths, especially those of the families Lymantridae, Eucleidae and Megalopygidae. Some of these, such as the European browntail (*Euproctis similis*) and the American puss moth (*Megalopyge opercularis*), have sharp spines which contain a toxin, capable of inducing fainting, nausea and other extreme symptoms. Obviously, reactions vary according to the individual's sensitivity, but rubbing of the eyes, even after handling some of the less well-armed hairy caterpillars, can have unpleasant effects in irritating the delicate eye membranes. These groups apart, the great majority of moth and butterfly caterpillars can be handled with complete safety, although some tend to be viewed askance simply because of their ability to look like something else. I have known the 3-inch (7.5 cm) caterpillars of the elephant hawk-moth (*Deiliphila elpenor*) to be taken for small snakes, principally because of the eye-like markings on the anterior part of their body. A host of flies, beetles, moths and other insects tend to be avoided like the plague because of their highly effective imitation of the shape, colour pattern and even behaviour of bees and wasps, while insects with long ovipositors are regarded with equal suspicion, just as harmless dragonflies are still often thought capable of stinging. Scarlet cardinal beetles (*Pyrochroa* sp.) are colloquially called 'blood-suckers' in some parts of England, simply, it seems, on account of their colour.

The true blood-suckers of the insect world tend to be far more subtle both in appearance and habits, and include mosquitoes, midges (Ceratopogonidae), fleas, lice, horse-flies, tse-tse flies, black-flies (Simulidae) and certain bugs, such as the bed-bug (*Cimex lectularius*). By transmitting the micro-organisms that cause malaria, yellow fever, bubonic plague, typhus, and other diseases, insects like these have caused infinitely more trouble to man than any other animals, large or small, in those countries where such contagions are endemic. Elsewhere, the effects of bites are not usually serious and seem to depend on the individual sufferer. Some people are far more sensitive than others to the saliva and anti-coagulants such insects inject and may display heightened symptoms, especially if they are allergic or anaemic. As I know from personal experience, it is, moreover, a source of (literal) irritation that one member of a group may be subject to almost constant attack from mosquitoes, midges and horse-flies, while his companions escape almost scot-free. Those, like myself, who perspire unusually freely inevitably give off heightened chemo-tactile 'messages' in the form of heat, moisture and carbon dioxide which attract the insects like a magnet. In many vampiric insects it is only the female that takes blood, largely because such a meal is essential for the proper maturation of her eggs. In others, notably bugs and lice, both sexes, as well as larvae feed on human and other animal blood. There are, curiously enough, even some moths that suck blood. One of them is the south-east Asian *Calpe eustrigata*, which commonly attacks cattle, buffalo, antelope and deer with a proboscis which has evolved from the more usual nectar-drinking role into one that is quite capable of piercing tough mammalian hide.

Other much dreaded invertebrate stingers and biters belong to the same class as the spiders (page 78), and of these the scorpions are the most feared. Most, however, are small, shy and nocturnal in habit, and the only real danger from them comes when they are trodden on barefoot. Apart from the USA and Mexico, where it is said there are regularly more fatalities from scorpion stingings than from snake bite (and that includes rattlesnakes), these arachnids are not generally troublesome, although some species do display a disconcerting tendency to make their way into houses and shoes. Europe has few species, and Britain no native ones.

One tiny (40 mm) species (*Euscorpius flavicaudis*) has managed to establish itself in parts of Essex and Kent, as a result, it seems, of inadvertent importation via container lorries from the Continent, but it is unaggressive and its sting can scarcely pierce the skin.

Centipedes are another group which frequently figure in people's ideas of the acme of nightmare loathsomeness. Afforded a zoological class all to themselves (Chilopoda), they are distinguishable from the commonly confused millipedes (Diplopoda) by the possession of a single pair of legs on each body segment, whereas millipedes have two. Centipedes, unlike millipedes, are carnivorous, and while none is aggressive to man some large species, like the 6–8 inch (15–20 cm) *Scolopendra heros* of the south-west United States deserts, are capable of inflicting a painful bite by means of their specially adapted, toxin-injecting forelegs. However, as with so many small animals, it is only deliberate handling or interference that would induce such a reaction.

Apart from the insect 'vampires' referred to earlier, leeches are probably the only invertebrate animals to actually seek out and, as it were, prey on man. Even so, they are the subject of widespread misapprehension. Because of their principally aquatic nature, leeches do not number man very highly in their lists of hosts unless he happens to be trekking through tropical jungles. Tales of men being drained of blood or killed by these earthworm-relatives are dubious to say the least, although the cumulative effect of a number of leech suckers (each capable of withdrawing about 10 cubic centimetres of blood at a sitting) would certainly be weakening, apart from the possibility of introducing pathogenic micro-organisms via their saliva. In any case, by no means all leeches are parasitic. The hoary old belief that half a dozen European horse leeches (*Haemopsis sanguisuga*) can kill a horse is wildly astray, since the species feeds solely on small invertebrates and cannot suck blood at all!

EARWIGS

Earwigs would appear to hold a rather special place in people's disaffection, principally because of the widespread belief that they have a marked propensity for the human ear, and for this reason merit a discussion all to themselves. Their very name implies some connection of this nature and while, as we have seen elsewhere, popular names can be misleading and in themselves lead to and perpetuate misunderstandings about animals, of the basic mistrust that exists about these rather inoffensive little insects there seems no doubt. So far as I am aware, the belief is European in origin, referring principally to the common earwig (*Forficula auricularia*), a cosmopolitan species which, together with its lore, has found its way into Africa, the Americas, Australia, New Zealand and Japan. Cautionary tales, short stories, verses and, of course, grass-roots belief itself, supposedly linked to age-old tradition, all tell of the earwig liking nothing better than to crawl into the human ear, burrow inside and, horror of horrors, lay its eggs in the brain!

The latter part of the notion, at least, is arrant nonsense, since it is doubtful if any earwig – even the giant (80 mm) *Labidura herculeana* of St Helena – would be capable of piercing the gristly ear-drum with jaws that are intended primarily for chewing waste matter or soft-bodied insects. Entry into the convolutions of the outer ear, leading to the tympanum, is, however, a different matter and there are a number of examples in the literature, as well as in doctors' case-books, of earwigs having to be extracted from the aural passage, where they have apparently succumbed to entombment in the cerumen, or ear-wax, which the ear probably exudes in greater quantity whenever there is an entry of some foreign body. To appreciate how and why such intrusions happen – which considering the species' abundance and liking for domestic situations is not often – it is necessary to examine the insect's nature in general. *Forficula auricularia* is clearly an example of regressive evolution in action. Despite the possession of a pair of large, delicate yet fully operative wings, it rarely uses them; indeed, very few have ever seen it fly, and then only for short distances. Principally a scavenger, it finds all its living requirements at a terrestrial level: beneath rubbish heaps, at the heart of vegetables and flowers and under moist peeling bark and large stones. It is a great creeper and crawler and, like many such insects, is strongly thigmotaxic, which means that it is happiest when as many parts of its body as is possible are in contact with some moist surface. Any position that is dark, moist and also warm would doubtless prove attractive as a temporary shelter, which probably explains earwigs' occasional entry into the ear, since it is significant that most such occurrences derive from people who have been sleeping on the ground. Indeed, it is possible that the more alarmist aspects of the belief originate from times when poorer people habitually slept in this position, perhaps on straw. It is hardly necessary to say, of course, that earwigs do not deliberately seek out the ears in preference to other suitable sites. Neither would they be likely to use them as more than temporary retreats. On the few occasions when they have had to be surgically extracted, it is probable that the natural human reaction to the entry of a foreign body in the ear – poking a finger in – has resulted in the intruder's injury, rendering its retreat impossible; the cerumen completing the job of imprisonment.

To be quite fair to those who find it difficult to shake off the belief, we have to say that there may be a little more to the matter than that. The

The French name of the earwig (***Forficula auricularia***) ***perce-oreille***, would seem to refer to the shape of the male's forceps which resemble that of the tool once used for piercing the ear lobe for earring suspension. (see p. 24.)

cerumen in the human ear has often been maintained as having a deterrent, even insecticidal property; however, if there is one thing that can be said about *Forficula auricularia* it is that it has an extremely undiscriminating palate. It will consume all manner of waste substances, including fragments of soap in the bath, and in my experience is not above chewing at the fatty tissue at the base of human hair follicles. I would be the very last person to wish to seem at all scare-mongering so far as insects were concerned, yet one wonders if the occasional earwig might actually find cerumen to its liking and thus progress deeper into the aural passage with a view to satisfying its individual taste!

Considering human populations and the vast numbers of tiny insects always around us, it would be surprising if the latter did *not* occasionally find their way into our ears. Thus it is that earwigs are by no means the only insects to intrude in this way. A correspondent of mine told of once having a 'tiny midge-like creature' extracted from her ear, where its presence had sounded like an underground train. In the summer of 1984 a boy holidaying in a log cabin in the wilds of Scotland suffered an even more alarming experience when a large ground-beetle made its way into his ear, necessitating its removal by micro-surgery. Obviously, such occurrences are very far from typical but they make it easy to understand how fears and prejudices arise and persist as folklore.

6·DANGERS, REAL AND IMAGINED

CRY WOLF

It is perhaps not altogether surprising that the image of the wolf as a dangerous, often rabid, man-eater persists. Every year, reports of wolf attacks on people, more especially in the mountainous regions of Central and Southern Europe (notably Italy and Greece) appear in the popular press, with only the vaguest substantiative detail. No-one suggests that such accounts are total fiction, yet it is equally clear that had they been subjected to close analysis a rather less alarmist picture would have emerged. A significant point about these reports is that they almost invariably occur in winter, for it is a known fact that severe weather may cause wolves to range wider in search of food and even raid livestock. The Anglo-Saxons called January *wulfmonath* for precisely this reason. The point is whether these great canids ever make it their business to unprovokedly attack man in preference to his domestic animals. Presumably they would retaliate if harassed or wounded, and they might not take kindly to having men get between them and their intended prey, but that is surely a rather different matter.

Defending the wolf is fraught with difficulty, for the plain fact is that people believe what they want to believe, or have been brought up to believe, and retain conceptions of animals which mere rationality may find impossible to change or even modify. The fictional theme of packs of wolves howling outside the cottager's door or relentlessly pursuing a *troika* through the snow is an ineradicable part of Central and Eastern European folklore, in particular. Every child is semi-indoctrinated with tales of the Big Bad Wolf and Little Red Riding Hood and, of course, werewolves (literally 'man-wolves'), while animal taxidermists of the past would scarcely have been thought to have done their job properly if they did not exhibit a stuffed wolf glaring and snarling horribly at the visitor.

In normal circumstances, it seems likely that wolves have always been shy of man, more especially today when they have learned to be wary of

88

his high-powered telescopic rifle. A solitary person caught in the midst of a hungry wolf-pack might well be killed and eaten, but it is equally possible that 'evidences' of such attacks – half-eaten bodies, with wolf tracks leading from them – have been made after the man had died from exposure or other causes. Attacks might also occur during intrusion on wolves' territory, especially in courtship situations or where young male wolves have become sexually mature and (like young male humans) more aggressive. To balance this, a number of people have overcome any traditional fears they might have and actually made friends with truly wild wolves, both in Europe and America, without ever being attacked. Farley Mowat, during a study of Canadian timber wolves, even went so far as to confront a she-wolf and her cubs in her den and survived to write about it in *Never Cry Wolf* (1972).

BIG CATS AND MINOR MENACES

Lions, tigers, leopards and other 'big cats' only rarely become man-eaters. When they do it is usually because they have been crippled by man and cannot hunt in their normal manner. In any case, we have no hang-ups about them. We respect their size and strength and, unless we are foolhardy, are happy to give them a wide berth, just as the ailurophobe avoids their rather smaller, domesticated relatives. A close confrontation with a brown, grizzly or polar bear, unexpected or otherwise, would probably be a serious matter for an unarmed man, for most can run at least as fast as he can, but he would be in no danger of being hugged to death. Bears do not kill in that way: they bite, and swipe with their massive paws. Provided we keep a respectful distance, bull elephants do not usually charge men, though one suffering from tooth- or tusk-ache (which must be painful indeed) might be rather more irascible. Most rhinoceros reactions of this kind tend to be sheer bluff, since the animals are short-sighted and often have the greatest difficulty in seeing precisely what it is they are pursuing. Gorillas, powerful though they are, are even less aggressive, though early travellers' tales tended to place them in a very different light (page 150). Kangaroos and giraffes can bestow a near-lethal kick, but one would have to wound and corner the creatures or be a very inexperienced zoo keeper to suffer it.

The largest marine mammals, the whales, are not dangerous to man, since most of them are plankton-feeders, lacking proper teeth. Of the toothed whales, probably only the great sperm whale or cachalot has a throat large enough to allow them to swallow a man and thus lend support to the Biblical Jonah episode, which is surely no more than a parable even if we translate 'great fish' into 'whale'. There are a number of latter-day reports of men being swallowed by sperm whales, or even

There have been reports of stoats and weasels (***Mustela nivalis***) attacking man when in family parties, but such behaviour is surely rare.

being recovered alive from their stomachs, but they are of doubtful authenticity, few and far between, and only 'likely' to happen in truly exceptional circumstances, as when one of a whaling party falls overboard. The so-called killer whale or orca (*Orcinus orca*) commonly ventures onto ice floes in pursuit of seals and penguins and is occasionally reported to have attacked man, although on other occasions the species has shown extraordinary forbearance in the face of great provocation from hunters. Cetaceans in general are infinitely more sinned against than sinning.

Some of the most interesting mammalian 'threat lore' emanates from smaller groups, such as stoats and weasels, which occasionally move about in family parties, more especially in autumn. There are a number of published accounts of gamekeepers and others being physically attacked or menaced by these little carnivores, but just how much of it is in response to the initial killing of one or more of the party it is not easy to say. What does seem clear is that, just as in man, animals wax that much bolder and more aggressive when in pack situation.

Many mammals make up for their limited size with defensive armaments which can make a human handler quickly drop them or suffer damage for his temerity. The Australian duck-billed platypus (*Ornitho-rhynchus anatinus*) – surely the most 'unlikely' of all mammals – has, in the adult male, a poisonous spur on each hind leg which can produce exceedingly painful effects. Some species of shrews have venomous bites, among them the European water shrew (*Neomys fodiens*), the American short-tailed shrew (*Blarina brevicauda*) and the very much larger *Solenodon paradoxus* of Haiti. There is no evidence to suggest that

90

ordinary common shrews are similarly armed, though they were long considered to be something of a minor menace to man and beast for this reason. It is possible that the belief arose from noticing that domestic cats, while killing shrews readily enough, hardly ever eat them because of their alleged musky flavour – and are immediately sick if they do.

FEATHERED FRIENDS?

Attacks from flocks of birds are solely the product of the fiction-writer's or film-producer's imagination. Such avian assaults as do occur are rare and are naturally likely to be most severe when very large species are involved, more especially when nests are approached. Ostrich cocks are said to be especially irritable during courtship and mating, and can inflict considerable damage with a blow from one of their immensely powerful legs; so, too, the related cassowaries of Australia and New Guinea, whose feet are armed with lethally sharp inner toes. Smaller birds, especially predators, may also prove aggressive in reproductive situations. One man walking beneath a tree containing a tawny owl's nest had his nose broken, his forehead gouged and his eye partially ripped open by an irate parent. Eric Hosking, the world-famous bird photographer, actually lost an eye as a result of a similar attack.

One of the most widely-believed bird dangers devolves upon the supposed ability of the mute swan (*Cygnus olor*) to break an arm or leg with a blow from its wing. These birds are certainly large, with a wing-span of some 6 feet (1.8 m), but their wings are light and hollow-boned, and it is doubtful if they could cause any serious damage. A young child, old person or one with weak bone structure *might* suffer a breakage from this cause, but it would surely be a freak occurrence even then. It is worth bearing in mind that those who have much to do with swans – swan-uppers, bird-hospital people, and so forth – must receive many blows without ill effect – or, if they do, we do not hear about them. In any case, while swans commonly put on a show of aggression when defending eggs and young, it usually consists only of much wing-flapping and hissing, rarely any attack as such.

Despite legends of the giant roc (page 126), it is unlikely that any bird has ever looked upon man as his natural prey. Tales of eagles carrying off young children, perhaps reinforced by the Ganymede legend, seem unverified, except in the solitary case of a white-tailed sea eagle (*Haliaeetus albicilla*) which in the eighteenth century is said to have carried off and killed a child in the Faeroe Islands. Eagles of this kind can carry weights of about 7–8 lb (3–3.5 kg), so it is *possible*, but the circumstances would have to be exceptional, to say the least, since these great birds have a deep mistrust of man and all his works – by no means surprising in view of the persecution of eagles that has taken place down the centuries. Perhaps the nearest thing we get to bird-man predation in temperate climates comes from ravens, carrion crows and magpies. Anyone lying totally helpless and paralysed in open country might be in some danger of losing his eyes to these large corvids, such delicacies being evidently high on their primarily scavenging list. Certainly, the only human corpse I have ever had the misfortune to discover in the open air (or elsewhere!) lacked eyes, undoubtedly from this cause. Whether this corvid foible is in some way linked to their fascination with bright objects in general, I cannot say, but an old countryman friend of mine tells me he thinks it may explain the first two lines of the well-known verse beginning 'One for sorrow, two for joy', about the varying luck imparted by the sight of magpies (*Pica pica*). One such bird could be unlucky because it would have a clear field of attack on any helpless victim, whereas two would immediately begin to quarrel over their prey. He tells me the idea stems from trench warfare in World War 1. I leave any assessment of its feasibility to the ornithologist!

MALIGNED AMPHIBIANS

It is probably true to say that much of the dislike of toads and, to a lesser extent, frogs that used to exist at grass-roots level has long since died the death. Shakespeare's reference to the toad as 'ugly and venomous' in *As You Like It* is surely nowadays only accepted in the purely literary sense; yet the notion of toads being deadly poisonous or that handling one was likely to induce the growth of warts were, at one time, beliefs very firmly and widely held. The numerous excrescences over all parts of the toad's body, plus its instant rejection by any dog foolish enough to mouth it, were sufficient to establish the animal's image in the eyes of the superstitious. Few in former times would have dreamt of handling *Bufo bufo*, but had they done so its frequent reaction in such circumstances would scarcely have been designed to alleviate such doubts. Held in the hand, a toad may well copiously empty its bladder, perhaps in nervous reaction, and if a small cut were already present on the skin this *might* have caused minor infection, if not warts.

Actually, toads (as well as frogs, newts and salamanders) *are* poisonous, if not venomous, which suggests the presence of venom-injecting mechanisms absent from the amphibia. Those wart-like protuberances on its body and more especially the large parotid glands just behind the eye contain an irritant substance which can be exuded in times of stress, notably when seized by a predator. Dogs and cats biting or worrying toads almost invariably suffer for their temerity, foaming at the mouth and even vomiting, and it seems likely that the toad's secretion has the effect of irritating the mouth's mucous membranes, especially since vomiting is sometimes also accompanied by blood. Some animals like badgers and foxes are said to be able to surmount the problem of the toad's indigestible 'peel' by literally scrubbing their victim's skin off before eating them. Snakes, probably the toad's principal enemy, have no such difficulty, since the amphibians are swallowed whole and the reptile's digestive system disperses any toxic effects.

Probably the only times when people are likely to experience any unpleasant reaction from the toad's secretion are when they happen to rub their eyes or lick their fingers immediately after handling numbers of toads, notably in 'road-rescue' operations. Then the irritation is reported to be rather like having pepper thrown in the eyes, and its taste bitter and acrid.

As mentioned, other amphibians, such as frogs, newts and salamanders, have somewhat similar defences, and some tropical species of frogs are especially toxic. Secretions in the skin of South American arrow-poison frogs (family Dendrobatidae) contain an alkaloid poison so powerful that natives of Brazil, Peru and Ecuador use it to tip their arrows. One species, *Phyllobates terribilis*, is said to be quite dangerous merely to touch. Clearly, those perpetrators of toad 'old wives tales' told rather more than they knew!

Some beliefs about amphibian malevolence are far more fanciful, though no less persistent, it seems. Ireland has no snakes to loathe, but locals make up for it by focusing their suspicions on their native newts (*Triturus vulgaris*) and lizards (*Lacerta vivipara*). The newt is, apparently, the Irish *Airc luachra* (also variously called *Ailp sleibhe*, *Ailp luachra* and *Eascu luachra*), which popular superstition tells has a tendency to creep into the mouths and down the throats of those sleeping out of doors on the ground. The lizard seems to have become tarred with the same brush over the centuries, and indeed the identity of the alleged intruder is not always clear even to those who still half cling to the belief. Only a year or so ago, a man from Ballyleary, County Cork, wrote in response to an article of mine to say that he had found the caterpillar of an elephant hawk-moth (*Deiliphila elpenor*), which locals told him might well be the *Airc luachra* and of particular danger to children. My correspondent added that he had found the caterpillar whilst digging near a stream and intended to keep his mouth firmly shut when engaged in such activity in the future, just in case the locals were correct! No comment is necessary, I think, except to emphasise that there is little danger of any animal — newt, lizard, caterpillar or *Airc luachra* — making its way into the body by this means, and certainly not without waking the sleeper, however much Irish whiskey he might have consumed.

CROCODILIANS AND OTHER REPTILES

Since crocodiles can attain a considerable size, cannot chew, and have little or no sense of taste, it is scarcely surprising to find that they do not always discriminate between man and their more usual mammalian, fish or bird prey. The Nile crocodile (*Crocodylus niloticus*) is among a number of species that are known to kill and eat man. Attaining a length of over 20 feet (6 m), it has slain or mutilated many a swimmer unwise enough to intrude on its territory. Nor can one be too sceptical of tales of native fishermen being chased and overtaken out of water, since these great reptiles can not only swim fast but put in a good turn of speed on land, as well. The widespread estuarine or saltwater crocodile (*Crocodylus porosus*), the only crocodilian occurring in the sea, and the Asian mugger or Indian crocodile (*C. palustris*), have also been responsible for human fatalities. New World crocodiles, alligators and caiman are not generally dangerous unless attacked first.

Apart from snakes (page 70), other reptiles are rarely dangerous to man. The Gila monster (*Heloderma horridum*), a slow-moving lizard of the deserts of the south-west USA and Mexico, can bestow an extremely painful venomous (neurotoxic) bite, while the snapping turtles (family Chelydridae) of the eastern United States and Central America need to be approached with caution because of their powerful, if non-venomous, beak-like jaws; yet, as in so many animal groups, appearances can be deceptive. To the unsympathetic eye, no more hideous monster could be imagined than the large South American matamata turtle (*Chelys fimbriata*), whose unmoving position on the river-bed somehow heightens the effect of its coruscated shell and beaked, almost deformed-looking, head. In fact, it is almost entirely benign and cannot even bite properly – merely opening its mouth and drawing in small edible items by suction, subsequently swallowing them whole.

TERRORS OF THE DEEP

Sharks, piranha fish, octopus, squid, even crabs – all have come in for more than their fair share of blame as man-eaters in fiction and film, with the first very much at the top of the list of villains. In fact, of the 350 or so known shark species, less than 10 per cent have ever been involved in attacks on people, and the majority of those have come from one particular species, the great white shark (*Carcharodon carcharias*), which has a wide distribution in warm seas throughout the world. These great fish certainly have attacked, and will continue to attack, swimmers, but it cannot be emphasised too strongly that they do not do so in preference to other things. Indeed, it has been suggested that most shark assaults come about because the aggressor is not always entirely clear about what it is trying to engulf. Sharks have excellent vision (even perhaps colour vision), but their senses of taste and smell are not highly developed, so that even totally inanimate objects are likely to be swallowed if they seem like potential prey. That sharks develop a taste for human flesh and deliberately seek out man for this purpose is thus arrant nonsense. The size of the great white has also been the subject of gross exaggeration. Most rarely exceed a length of about 20–25 feet (6–7.5 m) and while there are inadequately substantiated reports of 'monsters' approaching 40 feet (12 m) it is unlikely that any ever attain the size of those beloved by film-makers.

Since the great white shark is somewhat unusual among the Lamniformes in occasionally frequenting shallow waters (most other species are more pelagic), it has naturally tended to cause most problems to man around warmer coasts with a high population of bathers, such as Australia and California. Elsewhere, attacks are exceedingly rare. Some sharks occasionally occur in European waters, even near the coast, but (once again) appearances can be deceptive. The forbidding-looking basking shark (*Cetorhinus maximus*), for example, can attain a length of some 36–39 ft (11–12 m), and displays the characteristic dorsal fin so conducive to panic reaction in the observer. In fact, it feeds solely on plankton.

Other, much smaller fish have also been the subject of much scare-mongering, and it is not always easy to be sure where fiction ends and fact begins. Piranhas (*Serrasalmus* spp.), about eighteen species of which occur in the rivers of South America, are a prime example. Horror stories, notably those with a revenge theme, tell of human victims being first gashed and then thrown into a river, after which the piranhas, attracted by their blood, swarm in and strip the unfortunates to the bone. On the other hand, many an explorer has told of fording piranha-infested waters without any trouble whatsoever. Probably few species are dangerous. Some are certainly known to be herbivorous, consuming fruits that fall into the water, and others are at least partly scavengers or predators on other small fish. Clearly, much depends on which species happens to be encountered. One to be avoided, it seems, is the 14-inch (35-cm) red piranha (*Serrasalmus nattereri*), which is capable of snapping off a gobbet of flesh with each bite of its immensely sharp pointed teeth *and* lives in large shoals.

The candiru (*Vandellia cirrhosa*) is another Amazonian fish that might present something of a hazard to intruding man, and in a most unpleasant fashion. This tiny, match-thin relative of the catfishes is principally parasitic on other fish, whose blood it sucks after penetrating their gill-chambers. Unfortunately, it varies this habit with a penchant for human urine and has been known to make its way into the urino-genital orifices of those entering the water without proper protection. Since these pigmies of the fish world have erectile, backwardly-directed spines on their heads which make it virtually impossible for them to retreat by the way they came, they are horrors of the deep, indeed!

Very few other fish are dangerous to man in the sense of their taking the initiative in aggression. The so-called electric eel (*Electrophorus electricus*), which occurs in the rivers of Brazil, Colombia, Peru and other South American countries and is really closer to the carp than to eels, is capable of discharging an electrical voltage sufficient to stun a man and other large animals at a distance of several yards. Other electric fish, such as the electric catfish (*Malopterurus electricus*) and the marine electric or torpedo rays (*Narcine* and *Torpedo* spp.) emit much lower voltages, dangerous only to children or those with weak hearts. A combination of defence, predation and direction-finding would seem to comprise the main purposes of the fishes' electricity.

Deliberate interference probably accounts for nearly all other alarmist stories where fish are concerned. Conger eels (*Conger conger*) may attain a length of 9 feet (2.7 m), with a vice-like bite to match, but never attack man unless bearded and goaded in their rocky crevice lair beneath the sea. Many fish have toxin-bearing spines, fins and tail which can cause agonising pain if their possessors are trodden on with the bare feet. Weever-fish (*Trachinus* sp.), stone-fish and scorpion-fish (Scorpaenidae) come into this category and are not always easy to avoid since they habitually lie at the bottom of shallow seas and coasts, where their cryptic shape and pattern make them difficult to pick out. Sting-rays (*Dasyatis pastinaca* and others) have a flexible tail armed with poison-bearing spines which they are not slow to use in defence. They can also attain a large size, if nowhere near that of their giant relatives, the manta rays. To look at, these latter would seem the very archetype of deep-sea horrors; indeed, their strange bat-like shape, complete with 'horns' (formed by the pectoral fins) and typical ray tail, together with a size that in exceptional specimens may extend to 60 feet (18 m) across, has led to their being colloquially called 'devil-fish' and 'sea-vampires'. Both are misnomers since, like the basking shark mentioned earlier, the manta ray is truly a gentle giant. It is not even a danger to other fish, except minute species or young ones, for its reduced, flattened teeth render the manta incapable of doing more than browse on the seas' almost limitless harvest of animal and plant plankton.

With the exception of sharks, probably the most maligned and feared of all deep-sea creatures is the octopus, which popular opinion commonly confuses with squid, a very different animal, though both are molluscs. Occasional reports of truly giant octopus could well be true (page 132) but tales of these rather shy cephalopods attacking ships and fishermen, and even capsizing their boats, à la Jules Verne, are almost certainly fabulous. Octopus can certainly use their multiple suckers to grip and hold onto their prey with considerable tenacity, but the idea of their being able actually to strangle victims with their 'tentacles' (more accurately, arms or legs) is false. Octopus kill with their horny beaks, with which they inject a paralysing poison. Many octopus species are, in fact, only a few inches across their fully extended arms and, paradoxically, one of these, the Australian blue-ringed octopus (*Hapalochlaena maculosa*) *is* dangerous to man, if only when handled. Occurring all round the Australian coast, in rock pools and caves, it has a near lethal neurotoxic bite, which it uses both to overcome prey and defend itself. Fortunately, its contrasting yellow and blue markings make it highly conspicuous and therefore easily avoided.

It is likely that the majority of sailors' and fishermen' yarns concerning supposed octopus attacks actually refer to giant squid (*Architeuthis* sp.), since the latter's benignity is perhaps rather more open to doubt. Some individual squid can attain an enormous size, even accounting for popular exaggeration. Specimens 60 feet (18 m) long are well authenticated and estimates have postulated others up to five times that length. Assaults on fishing boats and even larger vessels are on record but evidence indicates that they have almost always been as a result of initial harassment. Invertebrates though they are, squid are intelligent animals, with a wide range of highly developed sensory and 'emotional' responses, so it is not unlikely that they would react violently to the use of harpoon or rifle against them. By and large, giant squid can scarcely be considered a serious threat to small-boat fishermen, since they generally live far out in the oceans at considerable depths. Nor is there any evidence that squid have ever attacked men in the water.

One completely sedentary mollusc that tradition has long regarded with deep suspicion is the giant clam (*Tridacna gigas*, and other species). Occurring principally on the coral beds of the Indo-Pacific region, these bivalve relatives of the oyster can attain a length of 4 feet (1.2 m), but their sole object in life is to affix themselves to the ocean bed and filter air and minute items of food from the water by means of their dual-acting gills and constantly waving cilia. During this rather passive activity, the two valves of the clam's shell are opened to varying widths, and when closed fit with such tightness and strength that anyone standing on the inner mantle *could* find his leg immovably caught and drown as a result. However, one would have to be either exceedingly careless or bent on suicide to manage it, since the 'lips' close exceedingly slowly, displacing many gallons of water. Moreover, the whole organism is highly conspicuous, with brightly coloured, usually purple and rich green, lips. Tales of pearl-divers being caught by these great shellfish may be substantially true but they are surely rare, and it is probable that the men (or women) involved have initially been in trouble from other causes. The plain fact is that considerably more danger is likely to proceed from very much smaller molluscs, among them coneshells (*Cionus* sp.) which occur in the same region as the giant clam. Notable for their exceedingly handsome shells, which are consequently much prized and collected, living coneshells can inject a most unpleasant nerve toxin with their rasping radula or 'tongue'.

With jellyfish, too, it is once again principally the smaller species that present the most hazards to man. Huge species of *Cyanea*, which have occasionally been reported as the size of a table-top and seem to have formed the basis of one of Conan Doyle's Sherlock Holmes stories, may occasionally become stranded in tidal pools but are normally found only in the open seas. They do not, in any case, sting anything like as violently or painfully, and sometimes fatally, as smaller species commonly called sea-wasps (*Chironex* spp.), widely regarded as the most venomous of all the Coelenterata. Fortunately, sea-wasps occur principally in warmer seas, whereas another, rather better-known member of the group, the Portuguese man o'war (*Physalia physalis*) occasionally ventures onto the shores of colder countries, sometimes in such numbers as to prompt official warnings on beaches. Actually, *physalis* is not a true jellyfish at all, but a community of hydroid animals functioning as one, although just as in jellyfish their stinging tentacles are used principally for stunning fish and invertebrate prey. Stings on humans are invariably accidental.

Tales of crabs attacking and devouring man are almost certainly purely fabulous – linked perhaps to their portrayal in giant form in horror stories and films. Crabs are almost entirely scavenging in their habits and giant crabs, swollen to man-size or beyond, simply could not exist for reasons that have been mentioned elsewhere with special reference to insects (see page 47). Some spider crabs – the Japanese *Macrocheira kaempferi*, for example – measure as much as 12 feet (3.6 m) across the outstretched legs and claws, but unfortunately for the fantasist can only live at ocean depths where buoyancy compensates for their bulk and weight. Even here, they would be unlikely to attack man without prior provocation. Certain Red Sea robber or coconut crabs (probably *Birgus latro*) have been accused of eating people, while the island of South Trinidad, some 700 miles (1,125 km) off the Brazilian coast, is said to harbour a colony of particularly malevolent man-eating land crabs – making life difficult for those seeking the legendary treasure of the pirate Captain Kidd, which tradition tells is secreted there! Such stories can only be regarded with deep suspicion. The crabs might well pick at any partially-decomposed bodies they came across, but one rather doubts if there is anything more to it than that.

7·AN ANIMAL *MATERIA MEDICA*

A HEALTHY RESPECT

There can be little doubt that wild animals are, on the whole, very much fitter and hardier than modern man, even without the latter's vast range of antibiotics, analgesics, sedatives, and the most up-to-date surgical techniques. Except when menaced or manipulated by *Homo sapiens*, they suffer remarkably little from physical injury or disease, and even less from stress. When they do succumb to these things, suffering is not generally prolonged, since their weakened state renders them liable to a quick death from predators. Moreover, since accident and disease are more likely to occur in older, less vigorous individuals, it is probable they were nearing the end of their natural life-span in any case.

Even in straightforward kills of healthy individuals, it is doubtful if the victims have either the time or the intellect to formulate regrets, or indeed any thoughts at all, about the matter. Indeed, it is not impossible that they 'feel' next to nothing during this brief passage to oblivion. Many animals certainly seem able to fall into a kind of cataleptic trance or self-hypnotic state when seized by a predator and others, after an initial outcry, resign themselves to their fate with scarcely a struggle. It is now thought that such a highly 'sensible' reaction may come about through the release into the tissues of substances called endorphins, which reduce the ability of the nervous system to pass pain messages to the brain. Man himself may have shared this ability with animals at one time but, with some notable exceptions, now displays it to a far lesser degree, probably as a direct result of his heightened intellectual and imaginative powers that, in turn, induce irrational fears and all manner of other emotional responses which animals generally lack and are indeed better off without.

Nor is animals' superior fitness solely physiological. They are fitter because they are adapted to existing in a particular type of environment and habitat from which, unlike all-intrusive man, they rarely stray. They are not prone to cerebral hang-ups such as man suffers from crowding together in high-rise flats, doing boring jobs or striving for better pay. Their lives are concerned almost solely with the basic problems of keeping warm/cool, feeding, reproducing, and dying without undue fuss, so that another generation may fill their place. Probably only man's earliest ancestors came close to this admirably simpler and happier way of life. Primitive hominids might have had a shorter life expectancy, but they were probably stronger and healthier, individually, and enjoyed a better balanced diet. In effect, man was, at this stage, really just another animal – which he is today only in the strictly biological sense.

Given all this, it is perhaps small wonder that man long tended to look at other animals with something akin to envy because of the beautiful, uncomplaining way they fitted into the scheme of life. Every animal must have seemed to him possessed of at least one attribute superior to his own: it might be more acute vision, greater running speed, amazing powers of copulation, reproduction or recuperation, longevity, or sheer strength. To try to assume these qualities by applying or actually consuming parts of such animals was perhaps a logical, if primitive step. In many cases, it was simply the animals' shape or appearance that suggested some improving possibility; in others, logic seems completely absent or inextricably mixed with ancient myth or ritual whose significance has been lost in the mists of time.

MEDICINAL MAMMALS

Much of the basic reasoning behind the use of mammalian extracts or parts in folk medicine would seem to be related to the original possessors' strength and supposed potency, especially those that possessed horns or tusks, vaguely suggestive of the erect male member. Thus, according to the early seventeenth-century English writer Rev. E. Topsell, powdered elephant tusk, perhaps adulterated with the burnt bones of dogs and fishes, 'corroborateth the heart and helpeth conception'. Deer horn (actually bone) might have a similar happy effect, while that of a young buck, boiled in its velvet, was thought for some reason to cure dropsy. Illicit trade in rhinoceros horn (again, not proper horn but compacted hair), a still more famous aphrodisiac and cure-all, continues today, although tourist demand seems now to have rendered its use rather more profitable for the manufacture of ornaments and dagger handles. In ancient China, a decoction of rhinoceros horn shavings was administered to women just before childbirth. Horns of all kinds, especially if they were thought to derive from the fabulous unicorn, were also considered of value for a very different reason: powdered, they formed an antidote to poison, or made into a cup detected its presence in a potion.

Other mammal parts were pressed into use, principally as charms but occasionally as potions. Asiatic physicians long recommended the invigorating effect of draughts derived from the teeth, claws and even whiskers of the tiger. In country districts of the USA the belief still persists that a bear's tooth serves as a charm against toothache and that sleeping on a bear-skin prevents or cures backache. Similar ideas of suggestion and transference doubtless account for the Old English customs of tying a horse's tooth around the neck of a teething child or of carrying a rabbit's foot against rheumatism or a sheep's patella (knee-cap) for preventing cramp: after all, these animals rarely suffered from such complaints themselves. Just why the carrying of a sheep's 'stitch-bone' (one of its molar teeth) should be valued as a charm against this arresting condition is less obvious, but it may somehow be linked to the tooth's shape, on the so-called 'doctrine of signatures' principle.

Mammalian fats and oils had a variety of applications, those of bear, rhinoceros and badger, for example, being held to be good for the treatment of hair conditions, including actual baldness. Badger oil, as well as its flesh and blood, was also used in the treatment of coughs, shortness of breath, rheumatism, and all manner of strains and sprains, while its skin was considered useful for those with paralytic disorders. The bone marrow of a horse was similarly recommended for loosening stiff joints and sinews, in contrast to hedgehog fat which was once, and perhaps still is, used by gypsies for cleaning their teeth. Roasted either enveloped in clay or simply spitted, hedgehog was considered delicate eating by these nomadic people, and little was wasted, since its blood, entrails, ashes and even dung were all pressed into use for various curative purposes, including as another hair restorative.

No-one has yet managed to come up with a truly effective cold cure, although 'neat's-foot oil' has long had its champions in this respect, especially among country people. To prepare it, you boiled and rendered down a pair of cow heels, adding a little lump of camphor to the resultant horn-derived oil. Massaged into the chest and back, such oil was said to be highly penetrating, providing much relief from congestion. It was equally recommended for the treatment of muscular complaints and was formerly, it seems, used to considerable effect by old-time boxing masseurs and seconds. John Ridd, hero of R.D. Blackmore's famous Exmoor novel *Lorna Doone* (1869), tells of relieving the pain of his aching ankles with the help of neat's-foot oil.

While derivatives of this sort clearly had some value, if only from the purely physical effects of their application, a whole host of other supposed cures are, like those mentioned earlier, so fanciful as to suggest that the patient would have required considerable faith in order to benefit from them, a degree of auto-suggestiveness perhaps comparable with the soothing effects of the modern placebo (literally 'I shall please'). Some that have survived in Europe right up to the present day prompt speculation because of their originally far wider and extremely ancient history of use. In parts of England and Scotland, for example, mice, roasted or fried, were offered as a treatment for a whole range of complaints, including whooping cough, colds, sore throats, quinsy and rheumatism, and might also prevent bed-wetting in children. Since not all medical or other lore is homespun, it is possible that such curious 'receipts' have their origins in the mouse's link with fertility, growth and disease-cure such as is found in the mythological creeds of Ancient Egypt, Crete, Greece and India, where mice were also often consumed medicinally. Equal mystery attaches to the ancient, originally classical, belief that the body of a shrew, burned and mingled with goose grease (page 111), constituted a sovereign remedy for piles, and that the tail of a live shrew, burned and powdered, reduced the sores resulting from dog bites. Probably the reasoning here is to some extent homoeopathic, since the common shrew was long thought to have a venomous bite and eating its substance might counter the effects of other poisonous conditions. In this connection, Gilbert White records in his *Natural History of Selborne* (1789) that it was common practice in the eighteenth century to wall up a live shrew within an ash tree, beneath which cattle, supposedly rendered lame by a shrew's bite, were made to pass or touch. Even people might benefit from such treatment and until quite recently children were still being taken to touch 'shrew-ashes' in the hope of curing conditions like whooping cough.

In a rather more active or positive approach to bronchial complaints, there is still a half-belief in some country areas of Britain in the therapeutic power of animals' very breath, more particularly in a confined space where a good old 'fug' had had time to accumulate. In Worcestershire, for example, anyone with whooping cough had merely to stand under a horse and let it breathe on him, presumably inhaling the equine's exhalations at the same time, to obtain a 'certain cure'. Unfortunately, not just any old horse would do: it had to be a skewbald for the treatment to work properly. At least it must have been a good deal safer than riding on the back of a bear, which was another recommended European measure for alleviating this distressing condition! My father recalls that in Buckinghamshire, at about the turn of the century, consumptives were recommended to go and breathe in deeply in the company of close-penned or hurdled sheep.

While the subject is not strictly medicinal, it is perhaps worth mentioning that mammals have also a long history as contributors to the production of cosmetics, their extraction often, sadly, accompanied by much cruelty. Musk, principally derived from the musk deer, civet (from the civet cat), castor (from beavers) and ambergris (from the sperm whale) are among a variety of extracts that have a long history of use for such purposes. Ambergris has, in fact, also had its medicinal applications. This curious substance, a concretion deriving from the whale's digestive tract, sometimes found washed up on beaches, is not only used in the manufacture of scent but has been found to have a certain proved value as a nervous stimulant. To balance this, it must be added that ambergris has also found its way into that long list of materials which eastern quacks recommend as aphrodisiacs.

SALUTARY SNAKES

Feared for their venomous bite, yet respected and even worshipped in mythology and religions the world over, snakes have long had an important part to play in primitive and folk medicine. Certain snakes were, as we have seen elsewhere (page 00), sacred to Aesculapius, the Greek god of medicine, but what would seem to be simply an association of ideas, linked to the reptiles' appearance and habits, has led to their more practical use. The first-century Greek physician Dioscorides, author of *De Materia Medica*, which remained a standard medical textbook in Europe until about the seventeenth century, was sufficiently impressed by snakes' smooth, unblemished skin, 'athletic' movements and lack of eyelids, suggestive of constant watchfulness and visual acuity, to write that the 'flesh of the viper, cooked and eaten, sharpens the sight, is good for nervous debility, and resolves scrofulous tumours'. He went

It seems probable that the device used by today's medical profession – a snake coiled about a staff – originally derived from the combat dance of the so-called Aesculapian snake (***Elaphe longissima***), sacred to Aesculapius, the Greek god of medicine. (See page 31.)

on to say that some believed that such a diet might also make the consumer live longer – a conceit presumably based on the snake's ability to 'rejuvenate' itself by shedding its skin whole during growth. According to Old Norse legend, wisdom and the gift of tongues might be imparted by eating snakes.

Galen, physician to the Roman emperor Marcus Aurelius, believed that a viper's bite was curable only by the application to the wound of a decoction made up of parts of the snake's body. Even as late as the turn of the century, adder fat and oil was still being sold by British chemists as a snake-bite cure, and snake-catchers made quite a good living by this means. The oil was also considered a remedy for bruises, black eyes and rheumatic gout and might be used against deafness. A snake's skin, worn inside the hat or bound about the temples, alleviated or even prevented headaches. Oriental apothecaries, both in Asia and in the West (for example, in New York and San Francisco), still sell snake potions for a whole range of physical and even psychological disturbances, among them impotence, which may have something to do with the fact that snakes are remarkable for the possession of *two* penes, or rather a double one.

INSECT STIMULANTS

It is somewhat paradoxical that the majority of insects used in folklorish medicine in the past were those capable of exuding, or whose bodies contained, some sort of irritant substance – among them ants, bees and various beetles. The principle behind their application was that of *counter*-irritation: by inducing varying degrees of excitation, perhaps even mild blistering, on the surface of the skin, congestion of those parts below the surface was relieved by stimulating blood-flow. Basically, the idea is perfectly valid and is actually employed in current medical practice, though little reliance today is placed on animal products. Many maintained, for example, that persistent skin complaints, such as lupus, could be cured by the application of ants' formic acid, or even that deep-seated articulo-muscular conditions like arthritis and rheumatism responded favourably to such treatment, more particularly when the acid was actually injected. The belief has long found grass-roots favour in western folklore and is equally mooted by a number of such primitive peoples as are still untainted by imposed 'civilisation'. The Bolivian Indians' championing of their ants' stings in the treatment of rheumatoid conditions has been regarded with such seriousness by Canadian medical authorities that in 1982 half a million of the ants in question were collected for research purposes. The Akawaio indians of Guyana use special ant frames for both initiation purposes and as a sort of circulatory stimulant, designed to make the 'patient' a better and more energetic worker, although the latter could owe something to sympathetic magic and the worldwide regard for the ant as an ideal of industriousness.

Bee venom, too, has found its curative supporters. Only recently, a Cumbrian gardener became so desperate for a means of relieving his rheumatism that he resorted to the painful ordeal of applying enraged bees to his sore and swollen joints, subsequently reporting a complete cure. The Russian Csar Ivan IV ('The Terrible') is said to have cured his gout by means of bee-stings – perhaps affording inspiration to certain modern Soviet physicians who, in 1984, were reported to be using live bee-stings in the treatment of rheumatism sufferers. Articular rheumatism is also said to respond favourably to the application of the proteinous substance called 'royal jelly', which hive bees feed to those larvae destined to be future queens.

The value of honey, both as a nutritious food and as a means of helping restore health, has long been recognised; so, too, has bee-collected pollen and a rather curious substance called *propolis*, which the bees use for building and repairing their nests. Vegetable in origin, this sticky, resinous substance has an exceedingly ancient history of medical use, dating back at least to 300 BC, and more recently claims have been made for its successful application as an anti-bacteriant and fungicide, in the treatment of rheumatism, and even as an anaesthetic.

One of the most interesting and controversial insect extracts is *cantharadin* or *cantharides*, derived principally from the so-called Spanish 'fly' or blister-beetle (*Lytta vesicatoria*). This extremely toxic material has long been recognised in unofficial circles and is still occasionally used in medical and veterinary practice as a superficial counter-irritant and blistering agent, as well as in the removal of warts and tumours and as a stimulative hair lotion. Beetles of this family (Meloidae), about 2000 species of which are known, have a worldwide distribution, and nearly all contain powerful acidic irritants, especially concentrated in the elytra or wing-cases, which in nature deter predation by other animals. Species of *Myalabris* are said to contain higher amounts of cantharadin than *Lytta*, and it seems probable that it was these, rather than the central and southern European *Lytta vesicatoria*, that Hippocrates and Dioscorides describe as the cantharides of the Ancient Greeks and Romans. *Myalabris cichorii*, an Asiatic species of blister-beetle, was used until quite recent times as a blistering agent in parts of India and China.

Cantharadin's application in western medical circles is now almost entirely superseded, despite its continued listing in many a pharmacopoeia and medical dictionary. Elsewhere it is probable that its popularity, for the purposes mentioned, continues unabated, as does its use in an

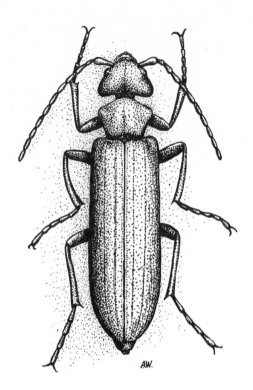

The blister-beetle (*Lytta vesicatoria*). Actual size c. 20 mm.

infinitely more doubtful, esoteric context. Taken internally, as a 'love philtre', it may be doubted if cantharadin increases either desire or sexual performance, despite a long history of its championing in this direction, more especially in the Middle and Far East. It does, however, induce certain physical effects, particularly spectacular in the human male, which probably explains why the substance is still much sought after by those of a concupiscent disposition. Taken internally, cantharadin irritates the bladder and urethra, this in turn inducing prolonged priapus (erection), rather as sometimes occurs in certain urino-genital disorders. The problem is that ingestion of the substance can have other, far more serious side-effects, such as internal bleeding, permanent kidney damage and circulatory failure, sometimes leading to death. Doses as small as 1½–3 grams have been known to produce lethal results, so it is certainly not a substance to trifle with. Fortunately, cantharadin is now virtually impossible to obtain over the counter, while its original insect possessors are either very locally distributed or identifiable only by the entomologist.

Extracts or decoctions made from other insects are generally far less severe in effect and really fall into the category of sympathetic medicine,

106

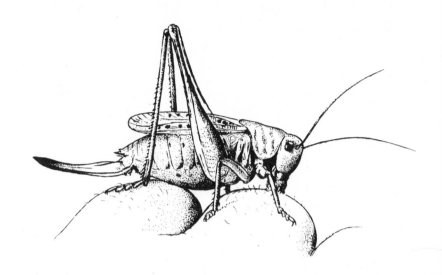

The European wart-biter bush-cricket (*Decticus verrucivorus*).

with no proven benefit (or harm) to the patient whatsoever, except perhaps via auto-suggestion. The earwig's supposed propensity for invading the ear, or other vague association with our aural appendages, prompted its application in pulverized, liquid form as a cure for earache. Other useful 'essences' might be obtained without harming the insect at all. The European 'wart-biter' bush-cricket (*Decticus verrucivorus*) was, as its name suggests, formerly used by country people to bite and supposedly reduce warts. These large grasshopper-relatives exude a black fluid – presumably a digestive enzyme – during serious biting, and until the eighteenth century, at least, Swedish peasants believed the liquid possessed the power to make the excrescences disappear. So far as I am aware, no-one has made any serious scientific investigation of the matter.

ALL-PURPOSE SPIDERS
So far as folk medicine is concerned, spiders might be said to come into the category of cure-alls since, at one time, in Europe at least, they were liable to be recommended for just about any of the ills that flesh is heir to. Swallowed whole, made into pills, or even spread juicily on bread and butter, large species were, in eighteenth-century Britain, firmly prescribed as a cure for fevers, gout, jaundice, digestive disorders, and even leprosy.

Running of the eyes might be stopped by the excreta and urine of a spider, perhaps mixed with oil of roses or saffron. Confined in a small box and hung about the neck, a living spider was held to have the power of drawing off the ague (malaria) into its own body, and might even prevent the wearer contracting it or the plague. Species like the common garden spider (*Araneus diadematus*) were considered of especial value, since the cross-like pattern on their abdomen lent sanctity to the proceedings, and they were also believed to contain a stone of special curative value.

Spiders' webs, too, have long had a place in rustic medicine, and for rather more logical reasons. There are probably still a few old countrymen who use a piece of web to staunch the flow of blood after having cut themselves, my own grandfather being one who did not hesitate to employ the same ready-made means. In most cases, the procedure merely involved the web being held against or bound about the wound, so that the effect was purely mechanical, in assisting the blood to coagulate, although other do-it-yourself first-aiders went so far as to actually *rub* the wound vigorously with the web, which half suggests the silk has some additional curative property of a chemical nature. Just how often such benefits as might have been obtained by web application were accompanied by subsequent blood-poisoning it is interesting to speculate. Doubtless the collector endeavoured to obtain the cleanest and freshest web available, but there must always have been a risk of introducing minute fragments of web-caught insects into the wound. Perhaps country people were hardier in those days.

The garden cross spider (**Araneus diadematus**). Slightly enlarged.

LEECHES

The idea that all manner of human bodily complaints could be alleviated by drawing off a quantity of blood is of exceedingly ancient origin, and the use of leeches to this end is scarcely less so. These blood-drinking relatives of the earthworm are known to have been part of the stock-in-trade of Greek and Roman physicians from at least the second century BC, but their employment in India, Arabia and Persia, and probably elsewhere, goes back much further still. Later medical practice tended to slavishly follow the example of the ancients and in mediaeval Europe, including Britain, the medicinal leech (*Hirudo medicinalis*) became so popular as a simple and virtually painless means of 'bleeding' that their human administrators themselves became known as leeches, and many people bearing the name 'Leech' or 'Leach' today can probably number one of these early medical practitioners among their ancestors. Nor did later advances in medical knowledge quickly render leeches obsolete and they were still in widespread use, and often specially and extensively bred, in countries like Britain, France, Germany, Hungary, Turkey and Russia, as well as exported to the USA, until well into the twentieth century. In just one year, 1863, it is estimated that seven million leeches were used in London hospitals alone.

Even today, the humble leech is not entirely scorned by the medical profession and, in a curious mixture of the primitive and the highly sophisticated, has been found especially useful in assisting the most up-to-date techniques of plastic- and micro-surgery. One of the major problems encountered with skin-grafts is that the blood's normally vital clotting reaction tends to work against such operations by inhibiting the fusion of the graft with the area of flesh to be covered. Leeches can help here since when they feed they inject an anti-coagulant which, by actually stimulating blood-flow, helps the graft to take more readily. Current medical practice also sometimes employs leeches for reducing gum-boils, ulcers and severe bruising, more especially in the region of the eye, where their removal of coagulated blood and plasma relieves pressure on the eye-ball in a delicately precise way that is difficult to match by surgical means. More squeamish patients may not always be too happy about being used as leech 'hosts' in this way, but one additional advantage of their application lies in the fact that the leeches' feeding is almost totally painless. While a single leech is capable of withdrawing up to eight times its body weight in blood, its presence is scarcely felt, except as a faint tickling, probably because skin lesion and sucking is accompanied by the injection of a natural anaesthetic which, in free nature, would prevent its too early detection and removal by an equally unwilling animal host. Clearly, leeches are among the few entirely valid success stories so far as 'medical animals' are concerned, the revival of interest in them being such that many hospital pharmacies now maintain a small stock of leeches for emergency use, obtaining them from registered breeders.

As mentioned earlier, old-time leech application tended to be far more indiscriminate, and almost any condition that the practitioner felt unable to treat in other ways prompted their liberal administration, in an attempt to rid the patient of his or her 'evil vapours'. Not infrequently, sufferers were bled so intensively by such means that they died from sheer weakness and loss of blood or through cross-infection of the wounds caused by the suckers. Moreover, while it was customary to make the leeches disgorge any previous blood meal by immersing them in vinegar, brine or camphor water, one doubts if the precaution was invariably taken, which meant that there was also probably an additional danger of the introduction of pathogenic micro-organisms picked up by the parasites from previous animal or human hosts. The problem does not arise today since the leeches are used only once and previously starved.

In Britain, during the past hey-day of leeching practice, large numbers of leeches were actually collected in the field, one method being to wade barelegged in ponds and allow the animals to affix themselves to the flesh. *Hirudo medicinalis'* rarity as a wilding in the British Isles today renders the method no longer feasible, although over-collecting is probably only one factor in its current decline. Others would seem to be the loss of its pond habitat, as well as the increasing scarcity of amphibians such as the common frog, which constitute some of the parasite's favourite hosts, when it cannot find mammals. Nowadays, the most tangible memory we have left of what was once a minor industry lies in the handsome decorated porcelain (delftware) jars in which the leeches were kept ready for sale in old chemists' shops.

MOLLUSCS AND OTHER INVERTEBRATES

A number of alleged aphrodisiacs have already been referred to, but they by no means exhaust the list. Oysters and whelks, in particular, are among a variety of healthful sea-foods still half-seriously considered to have a similar desirable effect in improving sexual performance. Norfolk fishermen and local traders, doubtless with an eye to increased trade, are fond of maintaining that the pleasures of a honeymoon are greatly enhanced by a good plateful of whelks, although there is little evidence to support their claim. Still less can be said of those improvers or cures which have terrestrial molluscs – snails and slugs – as their basis. I am not sure if the French penchant for *escargots* or Roman snails (*Helix pomatia*) renders them less prone to bronchial troubles, but a broth made from these and other snail species has in England long been recommended as a cure for colds, coughs and even tuberculosis. Such notions would seem explicable as the result of an association of ideas (the slime of the snails as against human mucus), and it may be supposed that something similar lies at the root of the suggestion that slugs be swallowed whole by those suffering from whooping cough. Others, among them the use of slugs against warts, are less fathomable and would seem to be all of a piece with the supposed ability of certain gifted people to actually charm these growths away by look, touch and a few muttered 'incantations'. Typically, a large slug is impaled on a thorn and as the slug shrivels and dies the wart slowly declines in size until it finally disappears. Some say that the slug, which in Britain is usually the all-black or orange *Arion ater*, must first be actually rubbed onto the excrescence and its slime allowed to dry.

Other invertebrates found their medicinal uses. Dried freshwater sponges were at one time in Europe used to rub on rheumatic joints, presumably on the counter-irritant principle since the powder contains fine spicules. An embrocation of the powder was also used as a cholera preventative. By contrast, the pill-like appearance and hard cuticle of those species of woodlice that roll up into a ball like the armadillo (their generic name is, in face, *Armadillidium*) suggested their use as cure-all pills, both for people and domestic animals. A similar association of ideas would appear to explain why these terrestrial crustaceans were sometimes hung in a little bag around the necks of babies to alleviate the pain of teething in infants. (See page 18.)

BIRDS, FISH AND REPTILES

Medicaments derived from birds, apparently not numerous, range from the purely fanciful to the wholly practical, with the emphasis very much on the former. The long-persisting recipe for improving the sight, or even curing blindness, which involved eating the heart, gall or other parts of an eagle, owl or raven, clearly related to these birds' own visual acuity. On the other hand, using goose-grease for rubbing on the chest of those with bronchial complaints must have owed at least something to the fact that a roasted goose always produces a large quantity of fat, and one might as well use it for something! With the use of doves' flesh, physically applied to draw out fever, we are again in the realms of symbolism and association of ideas (the reputed mildness of the doves' temperament as against the turbulence of a fever); and the same might be said of the old Yorkshire custom of consuming broth made from an owl for whooping cough – owls hooting, screeching and 'whooping' as they do with apparent impunity.

Fishes and amphibians present another mish-mash of ideas. Natives of the south-east African state of Mozambique still apparently firmly believe in the homoeopathic value of swallowing whole the gall-bladder of certain stonefish (*Synanceja*) as an antidote to its own poison, usually suffered when these perfectly camouflaged fish are accidentally stepped on (page 96). In certain islands of Polynesia, the eighteenth-century explorer and cartographer Captain Cook reported the local use of fish-skins for cleaning the teeth, the natives apparently maintaining that their oil also did much to prevent gum disorders. Nearer home, we find the Old English use of eel-skin garters to stave off rheumatism, while there was also some local past belief in the efficacy of the skin of a frog in curing warts, possibly because, unlike toads, it lacked these dermal outgrowths itself: a wart-free toad, in other words. The use of seahorses in the treatment of a whole range of complaints has an especially long history. Their ashes were originally recommended by Pliny as a cure for hot flushes, skin eruptions, baldness, and even the bite of a mad dog. Ancient Athenians used these curious little fishes' burnt substance, mixed with honey or pitch, as a poison antidote, although curiously enough the seahorse itself, steeped in wine, was regarded as being quite deadly. In sixteenth-century France, apothecaries offered seahorse ashes dipped in oil of roses for relieving chills and fevers. Today, their Chinese counterparts in American cities list powdered seahorse among their faster-selling aphrodisiacs.

Crocodiles, too, found early physicians' favour, notably in the eyes of the Rev. Topsell who, in his *Historie of Serpentes* (1608), assures us that their blood cured snake bite and restored poor eyesight, the juices of their cooked flesh helped wound recovery, and the dried skin acted as an anaesthetic when placed on a limb which required amputation. The reptiles' fat relieved toothache and various bites and was also good for 'wennes' — cystic tumours occurring especially on the scalp and face. All things considered, it is perhaps scarcely surprising that a stuffed crocodile was such a regular feature of old-time apothecaries' shops!

HEALING CONTACT

It is scarcely possible to leave this chapter, and all its highly imaginative medicinal lore, without some reference to the more truly beneficial, psychological and metaphysical effects which people may gain from living with animals — a topic which is rightly receiving increasingly serious attention from today's medical fraternity. Clearly, it was purely self-interest that first prompted man to domesticate animals like cattle, sheep and goats, but the keeping of animals purely as pets has a scarcely less lengthy history. The pre-Conquistadore emperors of Mexico kept snakes and humming-birds, the Chinese and Japanese crickets, cicadas and fireflies, while the many breeds of dogs and cats, most of them not expected or incapable of working for a living, are now so far removed from their wild ancestors as to provide an endless topic of speculation as to their origins. The Ancient Egyptians were doubtless

The Ancient Egyptians were extremely devoted to their domestic cats, which were sacred to their cat-headed goddess Pasht or Bast. This bronze effigy of a cat (dynasty unknown) is now in the Pitt Rivers Museum, Oxford.

happy that their domestic cats – probably derived from the African wild caffre cat, *Felis lybica* – were of such practical value in controlling the rats and mice in their granaries and homes, but they became so emotionally attached to them (even worshipping and deifying them) that when they died whole households would go into mourning and shave their eyebrows as a token of respect.

Clearly, there is something in the keeping of animals that satisfies a basic human need: perhaps a subconscious reaching out for the comforting contact with less physically and emotionally demanding creatures from whom man has contrived to separate himself in so many other ways. There is certainly evidence to suggest that such close associations are healthfully beneficial to man, possibly even to the extent of prolonging life. I am not sure I entirely agree with those who suggest that pet-keeping automatically makes people friendlier towards other people; in many cases, especially in those of an already somewhat introvert disposition, regular contact with animals can have the very opposite effect, in rendering human society less appealing. But there seems little doubt that concentration on the needs of a pet can take one's mind off personal troubles, while it may also, some medical people think, reduce stress and the possibility of heart attacks by keeping blood-pressure low. The purely physical benefits of having to take the dog for a walk are obvious enough, but many an old person must gain comfort and perhaps a new purpose in life through caring for the simple needs of a cat or canary, and receiving its (limited) affection in return. With this in mind, some hospitals are now allowing animals into old people's and children's wards, where they can be stroked and petted. The benefits gained from such contact, these enlightened physicans argue, far outweigh any risk of infection – which, in any case, is probably more likely to come from other people, including visitors!

All this, on the face of it, seems not far removed from faith-healing – which, in itself, may not be entirely without possibilities so far as animal contact is concerned. One woman with a long-standing arthritic condition, which had stubbornly refused to respond to years of standard medical treatment, actually claimed a cure from holding her cat's fur against her arthritic arm and hand. Was it merely auto-suggestion or could there have been sympathetic, healing communication between cat and woman? Less metaphysically, might there just possibly have been something in the static electricity generated in the cat's fur that worked such wonders? As yet, not even the wisest can say for sure.

8·LEGENDS, ANCIENT AND MODERN

THE PIED PIPER OF HAMELN

To see the townsfolk suffer so
From vermin was a pity.
Rats!

Robert Browning, *The Pied Piper of Hamelin* (1842)

Of the many narrative legends in which animals play an essential part, none is more famous than the tale of the Pied Piper of Hameln (correct spelling), immortalised for English-speaking peoples in Robert Browning's evocative poem but best known to Germans from the *Deutsche Sagen* (1816–18) of the Brothers Grimm. Certainly few present such intriguing possibilities of hidden meaning, for there are reasons to suggest that, in its basic elements, it may be rather more than just a mildly moralistic children's entertainment.

There are various versions of the legend, differing in minor details, but essentially the story goes that in 1284 the people of the small Westphalian town of Hameln were much afflicted with rats, which had assumed such unmanageable proportions that the town's chief burghers were more than happy to accept the offer of a strange piper, who suddenly appeared clad in old-fashioned pied or multicoloured raiment, to rid them of their rampaging rodents. Having agreed on a suitable monetary reward if he proved successful, the man set to work, inducing the rats to follow the seductive strains of his pipe and leading them straight into the nearby River Weser, wherein they drowned. Next day, however, when the piper returned for his payment, he was fobbed off with excuses and slights and offered a greatly reduced imbursement for his services. Such ingratitude not unnaturally angered the strange *Rattenfänger* who, now dressed as a huntsman, began to pipe to a different tune, leading all the town's 130 children over the age of four years, skipping and dancing in his wake, out of Hameln's East Gate to the foot of Koppelberg (also written as Koppenberg or Poppenberg) Hill, wherein piper and children disappeared, never to be seen again, except as a fabled race in Transylvania (now part of Romania), who subsequently could tell nothing of their ethnic origins. Some say the adults were at church while all this was going on; others that the distraught parents found themselves quite unable to move to their children's rescue.

The fascination of the Pied Piper tale lies in the fact that, stripped of its overlays of romanticism, almost every part of it is susceptible of plausible explanation, in which the rats and children may or may not be linked, if scarcely in the consecutive, narrative way the legend would have us believe. What is more, each has a certain measure of historical and documentary support, even if a good deal obscured by the passage of time. Taking the rat element first, the idea of someone being able to entice rats away in large numbers, whether by piping or other means, sounds ridiculous on the face of it, yet there are a number of factors which lend it, or at least the rats' evacuation *per se*, a certain plausibility. Firstly, we know that rats do migrate, often quite suddenly and in very considerable numbers (page 73), accompanying their concerted movements with much excited chirruping and whistling, which one modern writer has likened to the sound of a thousand starlings chattering in the tree-tops. The sounds apparently serve, at least partly, to attract other rats and may also be a form of pack-signalling designed to keep the concourse together. This, in itself, could easily have been transmogrified and fancified by much re-telling down the centuries into human-inspired decoyment. But it has also been suggested that a man with an inventive turn of mind and highly perceptive musical ear might have been able to construct a flute capable of imitating the rats' migration calls or notes. Some of the rats' communicative calls are, it seems, beyond the human auditory range, but even this does not render the idea totally outlandish when we consider the use of ultrasonic dog whistles.

Whatever else is speculation here, there can be much less about the figure of the rat-catcher himself, pipe-playing or not. Since rats were extremely common in mediaeval towns, where they caused considerable damage to basically wooden buildings and consumed and fouled large quantities of stored food, the peripatetic rat-catcher was a familiar and much sought-after personage in Europe during the period, and indeed continued in demand until quite recent times. (We are, of course, speaking of the black rat, which is much more of a house-lover than the brown: the latter in any case did not arrive in Europe until the eighteenth century.) Anyone who hit upon a wholesale method of rat control would doubtless have been made particularly welcome, which may account for similar if less celebrated tales of rat decoyment by pipers (and in some cases fiddlers) in other German towns, as well as in Austria, Persia and China.

One element which *may* lie behind the Piper legend, perhaps linking rats and children, is Bubonic or Pneumonic Plague which, as the so-called Black Death, reached Europe from Constantinople about 1347 and raged across the Continent for several years, breaking out again with slightly less virulence at other times during the fourteenth century. Directly responsible for slaying about a third of Europe's population over this period, we now know that this dreadful pestilence is transmitted to humans by the rats' fleas, more particularly when their original hosts die from the disease, thus prompting them to seek alternative (that is human) blood sources. Neither mediaeval Germans or anyone else at the time would have been aware of that vital link, so that we can dismiss any idea of the rats being decoyed away as a deliberate method of control for this specific reason (even supposing it were possible). Neither would simply decoying the rats into the Weser (some versions say a sough, that is a canal or sewer) effect their demise, since rats are normally excellent swimmers. However, one symptom of plague, both in rats and humans, is extreme thirst, so it is by no means impossible that Hameln's rats, humanly decoyed or not, might have made their way to the river in droves, drunk, and then succumbed.

Rat-conveyed plague could also suggest a pragmatic theory for the children's exodus. Since thousands upon thousands of young people must have been killed by it as it swept through Europe, the legend could be taken as a mere allegory: perhaps a veiled allusion to the children having been 'made away with' in numbers or to mass, plague-induced hysteria – epilepsy-like seizures or 'dancing' (comparable to the reference in the legend) being said to be one of the symptoms of Bubonic plague. That the children were singled out might also be explained by the possibility that such parents as had suffered from a milder bout developed immunity, whereas the children proved defenceless.

One sad social effect of the Black Death was, it seems, its disruption of family ties and affections, which often induced parents to abandon their children and leave their homes in order to escape its depredations. Could it be, one wonders, that Hameln's children banded together to escape parental neglect, or were they deliberately, but humanely, banished by their parents, perhaps in the care of a trusted leader? As a slight variant of this theory, some have opined that the piper's seduction of the children is really a euphemistic reference to a pogrom of the town's Jews, and perhaps exile of their children, as the supposed causers of the affliction. It is a matter of historical record that this much persecuted race often became the unreasoning targets of such blame, both in Germany and elsewhere.

Various other suggestions have been put forward to explain the legend's reference to the children's departure for places unknown, and some of them, such as the sudden collapse of a bridge whilst the children were crossing in numbers, strain the credulity as much as the legend itself. Others are slightly more plausible. One postulates that the young people's frenzied exodus can be interpreted in terms of an outbreak of manic dancing, comparable with the tarantism of mediaeval Italy (page 79). Whether such an explanation can be applied in this particular case is a matter for pure speculation, of course, but at least the phenomenon itself is well documented, with records telling of people in thirteenth-to fourteenth-century Germany suddenly taking to hysterical cavorting and singing together, despite professing to be in agonies all the while, until they frequently fell down and died. No satisfactory explanation has ever been given for such strange hyperactivity. Modern medical opinion suggests that it is unconnected with true St Vitus' Dance, which gains its name from the writhings of the unfortunate martyr whilst being subjected to torture, although it is interesting to note that true chorea is principally a children's complaint and also displays some of the symptoms of the mediaeval dancing mania. Still more seekers after the truth opine that the young people might have joined the so-called Children's Crusade (1212), led by a young man called Nicholas, or that they were induced to leave by foreign agents seeking settlers in eastern Europe. The latter is, again, backed by historical evidence, since in the fourteenth century there was indeed something of a large-scale exodus from Saxony, Westphalia and other parts of northern Germany to eastern Europe, notably Bohemia (Czechoslovakia). Might this explain the legend's reference to the children's resettlement in Romania?

It is characteristic of legends, and indeed has been made evident by what has been said so far, that the date of the alleged incident (or incidents) is very much a matter of opinion. The traditional date for the children's departure or abduction is usually given as 26th June, 1284 (St John and St Paul's Day), but is not backed by any factual evidence. Documentary references to the event itself, dating from the late fourteenth and fifteenth centuries, are both sparse and vaguely worded, while a church window, dated about 1300, and said to have recorded the children's departure, is long since lost. If we accept plague as an explanation of the whole affair, then this would suggest a rather later date for it than tradition allows. Various modern scholars, as well as the English writer and traveller James Howell (c. 1593–1666), who provided Browning with the basis of his poem, incline towards such a link. In a letter dated 1643 Howell reported that the legend was widely credited throughout Germany at that time, and that most believed it took place about 250 years before (that is, about 1390), which would thus accord with the plague theory. Howell also mentioned 'a great pillar of stone at the foot of the said hill, whereon this story is engraven' (a point borrowed by Browning), by which he may have meant a much later (1556) inscription. No such memorial now exists *in situ*, although there is an interesting tradition that a number of stone crosses (perhaps three) existed at the foot of Koppelberg Hill, to indicate the place where the town's children disappeared.

Whatever the facts of the case, and there is surely *something* behind it, the people of present-day Hameln rightly refuse to allow their world-famous legend to die. Every Sunday, from June to September, locals re-enact the incidents of rat and children decoyment, complete with adult piper and children dressed in mediaeval costume, with the latter also disguised as rats and mice. In 1984, a new stained glass window was installed in the town's Marktkirche to commemorate the 700th anniversary of the episode and replace the one so sadly lost. Thus does the passage of time serve to mellow what originally could well have been a far from happy event, rather as the seemingly innocent children's custom of singing and dancing 'ring-a-ring of roses' is believed to mask a darker secret of the English experience of plague.

WOLF-CHILDREN

According to ancient legend, the city of Rome was founded in 753 BC by Romulus who, with his twin brother Remus, experienced what must, to say the least, have been a rather unusual upbringing and childhood. The offspring of Mars, the god of war, and the erring vestal virgin Rhea Silvia, the boys were, it seems, made the innocent scapegoats for their mother's lapse by being cast adrift on the River Tiber, but were subsequently rescued by a she-wolf who suckled and raised them as if they were her own cubs. Later still, they were re-rescued and adopted by the herdsman Faustulus.

Mythical as the story may be, it is by no means unique. References to children being reared by wild beasts occur right down the ages, in myth, legend and purported fact. One of the best known concerns another pair of twins, Valentine and Orson, who are said to have lived during the time of Charlemagne (c. AD 742–814). Orson, we are told, was carried off by a she-bear and suckled along with her cubs, growing up to mingle human and bear-like characters by terrorising parts of France as the 'wild man of the woods', until reclaimed and pacified by his brother. There is also a long-standing legend of a monkey-child from Ceylon (now Sri Lanka), while of course Edgar Rice Burroughs' fictional tales of Tarzan, reared by chimpanzees, are well known. At a purely mythological level, there are innumerable tales of gods and goddesses, heroes and heroines, being similarly reared by tigresses, sows, goats and bitches, in China, Egypt, Assyria, Persia and Crete.

It is, however, the raising by wolves that is perhaps the most interesting aspect of the theme, simply because it recurs most frequently in traditional legends, right up to modern times, more especially in India. Kipling's delightful *Jungle Book* stories of Mowgli, the little Indian boy brought up by wolves, and assuming much of their ways, may not be entirely fanciful, since there is some evidence to suggest that such things may actually have happened from time to time. There are, in fact, several dozen reports of children being nurtured by wolves, even if few, if any of them, are entirely proved. The best documented would seem to be the case of two Indian girls, one aged eight, the other eighteen months, who in 1920 were apparently dug out of a wolf's den and found clinging in a tight ball to two wolf cubs. Their wolf 'mother' had, it seems, earlier been shot whilst trying to defend them. For this and the children's behaviour subsequent to human rehabilitation we have to rely almost solely on the diary of the Rev. J.A.L. Singh, who organised the dig and supervised the girls' teaching. This, Singh tells us in his diary, proved far from easy. At the outset, the little girls displayed all the attributes of wolves, crawling and even running on all fours, eating only raw meat, and howling, wolf-like at night: they also much preferred the company of other animals, especially dogs, to people, and generally it seems spent most of their time yearning for their lost wolfish existence. Even more incredibly, their eyes are said to have shone in the dark, as if they contained the tapetum, or light-reflecting layer typical of nocturnal animals. Neither, it seems, ever fully learned human ways and died within a few years of each other.

The Rev. Singh's fascinating account of the affair was subsequently published but has never been entirely accepted by wolf specialists or other zoologists. Critics argue that Singh's diary does not provide sufficient evidence that the children were actually *living* in the wolves' den, and indeed go further and suggest that they may simply have been maladjusted or autistic, thus 'explaining' their lack of response to human tuition. The truth will probably never be known until another such instance occurs and is properly observed and documented. What is surely unquestionable is that we cannot dismiss out of hand the possibility of wolves or other animals rearing children, if only because fostering of one animal's young by females of a quite different species is of fairly frequent occurrence, though admittedly the more bizarre of them occur in the highly artificial circumstances presented by zoos. It may seem unlikely that a basically carnivorous wolf would deliberately adopt a human child, but one can visualise situations where it might happen. A young child that had somehow managed to make its way into a wolf's den during the parents' absence might well, after playing with the cubs a while, become sufficiently impregnated with their scent as to be accepted as part of the family, more especially if the female were lactating and had lost some of her litter. It is worth remembering that very young children are often extraordinarily confident about approaching supposedly dangerous animals in a way that adults generally are loth to do: a large dog, for example, will commonly allow far greater liberties to be taken with it by a child than it would tolerate from men and women, who may be rather more inhibited, with perhaps past experience of being bitten, and thus show their nervousness. A complete absence of fear on the part of the child could well disarm our she-wolf entirely.

The only really puzzling thing about Singh's account lies in the presence in the wolf's lair of two children of such disparate ages. Were they sisters? Did the older one carry the younger and take it into the den with her? Or was it the wolves that took the initiative? There are certainly reports of Indian children being carried off from their homes by wolves every year, presumably, at least initially, for food, although their reliability is questionable, to say the least.

To return to the Romulus and Remus legend: those who have visited Rome will probably know that its citizens possess a permanent reminder of their city's fabulous origin in the form of a superb bronze statue of the she-wolf and twins, now on display in the Museo Nuovo of the Palazzo dei Conservatori. What is rather less known is that the item is really an amalgam. The she-wolf herself is believed to be Etruscan, dating from the sixth to fifth century BC, whereas the twins suckling from her were only added much later, by the Renaissance sculptor Pollaiuolo (c. 1432–98). There is some evidence to suggest that the wolf originally stood at the 'Lupercal', the reputed site of the wolf-den where the twins were reared. Apparently long maintained as a shrine, its actual position is, however, not known.

KING OF THE BIRDS

The lion, according to tradition, is the king of the 'beasts', and if there were any logic in the matter the eagle would surely hold that dignity for the birds. Legend, however, tells otherwise. The eagle seems to have had its chance of attaining the avian throne, but fluffed it or rather was beaten to it by means of a ruse, and that by a species at the other extreme of the size scale.

According to folklore, widespread throughout Europe, the story goes that the birds unanimously decided that kingship should go to whichever bird flew the highest. This the eagle then proceeded to do, but when it had reached the greatest altitude of which it was capable, a wren emerged from its feathers, where it had been hiding, and flew just that little bit higher, so gaining its end by decidedly unfair, if clever, means. The legend goes on to say, at least in some versions, that the eagle gained its revenge by dropping the wren from a considerable height or striking it with its great wing, so as to stub its tail feathers and render it incapable of flying higher than bush level.

Quite probably the tale is intended as a parable: to suggest that there is always hope for the little fellows of the world and that the big ones can be beaten if the former are prepared to use their intelligence, or even cheat. If, on the other hand, absolute extremes of feathered size are intended in the legend, then its perpetrators were inaccurate in their ornithology. The golden eagle is a majestic-looking species, and the largest European bird, but the wren is not quite the smallest. The British Royal Mint seems to have made just such a mistake when they chose the wren as the reverse design for the King George VI farthing, then the smallest denomination in circulation. The honour for avian diminutive-ness in Europe goes, in fact, to the goldcrest (*Regulus regulus*), which is altogether more regal in appearance than the universally brownish wren, since it bears a striking gilt-coloured, black-edged stripe down the centre of its head, suggestive of a crown, and is about a quarter of an inch shorter. Since one of the bird's alternative common English names is 'kinglet' (its scientific name means 'prince'), and it is also widely referred to as the golden-crested wren, although the two species are quite unrelated, one might be tempted to think that it was really the goldcrest that is referred to in the legend. Not so, it seems. Apparently folklore insists that it is indeed the wren (*Troglodytes troglodytes*) that won the crown, and it is a contention that seems to be borne out in most European languages, where the bird's colloquial names consistently reflect the element of royalty. The French call it *roitelet*, 'little prince'; to the Germans the bird is *Zaunkönig*, or 'hedge prince'; and there are many others with a similar connotation in Spanish, Italian, Swedish, Danish and Greek.

There is, however, rather more to the 'king of the birds' story than this, evidence which takes it out of the realms of pure myth and folklore, however charming, into that of semi-factual legend. Incredible as it may sound, it is well attested that small birds do occasionally hitch a ride on the backs of larger ones, and some of them have been goldcrests and wrens. There are a number of records of short-eared owls, in particular, carying goldcrests on their backs, notably when migrating, and at least one of a golden eagle bearing an unidentified small brown bird, probably a wren. Just how often this sort of thing happens, it is difficult to say, but it is quite possible that something of the kind – perhaps an eagle killed by an archer and subsequently abandoned by its tiny passenger – gave rise to the legend which most of us think of only as a moral tale or an encouragement to sharp practice.

THE ENTERPRISING HEDGEHOG

Hedgehogs (*Erinaceus europaeus*) have been accused of many things, some of them 'sinful', others merely intriguing. They are certainly known to steal the eggs of free-range poultry, and even young birds, having been trapped *in flagrante delicto*, but do they really suck the udders of cows, as the legend tells us? Many present-day farmers insist that they do and are not amused (as we might be) by the imagery the action conjures up since, they say, it is commonly accompanied by severe lacerations of the teats and by a substantial reduction in the cows' milk yield. As many householders will know, hedgehogs certainly enjoy a saucerful of milk, and there are records of individuals consuming more than a pint at a sitting, so if udder-sucking *does* happen the farmers' second point, at least, seems feasible enough.

At one time, zoologists tended to dismiss the farmers' suspicions as absurd, but there is now good evidence to show that the hedgehog's supposed propensity for taking a free drink from source is not merely fanciful folklore. For much of this we have to thank Dr Maurice Burton who, in his excellent monograph *The Hedgehog*, summarises observations of the activity and also refers to the findings of veterinary surgeons called in to treat the injured cows. The question is: how does the hedgehog manage it? Would such a little mammal really be able to grip and squeeze a cow's udder in its mouth and, if so, how does it do so without making the milk-producer start away in alarm? To the first, we can answer that a hedgehog's mouth gape is rather wider than might be supposed – some 1½ inches (4 cm); it is also perfectly capable of sucking milk from an artificial, udder-sized teat, as has been demonstrated experimentally. Getting at the udder in the first place equally presents few problems, it seems, even when the cow happens to be standing, since an adult hedgehog's stature is just sufficient for it to be able to stand on its hind legs, grasp the teat in its mouth, perhaps supported by the forepaws – and suck! There are, in any case, a number of field observations of hedgehogs milking cows, some of which were standing and others lying down.

To appreciate why it is that damage to the cow's udders sometimes occurs we must first realise that a hedgehog's dentition is both complete and impressive, as befits a virtual omnivore, although its canine or tearing teeth are not particularly well developed. Gentle pressure on the teat might suffice at the outset, perhaps, and effect no damage, but intense feeding pleasure together with a natural desire to increase milk-flow could well result in lacerations, as might a standing-feeding hedgehog that suddenly found itself toppling from its somewhat uncustomary, precarious position. Just how long a drink the hedgehog is allowed would presumably depend on both the position and disposition of the cow. One lying down might even welcome such attentions if it helped to

That hedgehogs (***Erinaceus europaeus***) *do* roll on apples seems clear. This illustration is from a thirteenth-century bestiary, formerly in Rochester (Kent) Priory and now in the British Museum.

relieve pressure on its bag, more especially, of course, since the hedgehog would be sucking under rather less strain and might not need to bite so hard and painfully.

Another hedgehog fable that seems, despite opposition from the sceptics, to be rather more than that concerns the animals' supposed habit of rolling on apples to take back to their lair. The theme is an extremely ancient one and there are numerous illustrations of it, in Old English bestiaries and in church carvings, all of them depicting the hedgehog walking along or lying on its back with small apples impaled on its spines. The point is: how do we explain it? We know that hedgehogs do eat fruit, in addition to a wide variety of invertebrate animals, as well as small mammals and nestlings, but the idea that they would deliberately roll on apples as a means of taking them home in quantity is very far from being universally accepted. One alternative explanation frequently offered is that apples might occasionally become impaled on a hedgehog's spines when falling from a tree, but this seems unlikely to be the answer since experimental attempts to spike apples by such means invariably fail: the fruit just bounces off the animal's short, criss-crossed prickles. Clearly, more concentrated pressure, together with a positive approach from the hedgehog is required to effect impalement, and this is precisely what observers claim to have seen. In most cases it seems that the hedgehog first collects a pile of the fruit, either by nosing them along or (if small enough) carrying them in its mouth, and then vigorously rolls on them several times, apparently in order to affix as many as possible. To back such observations up, 'nests' of apples have been found, or trails of them leading from the trees, many of them displaying small perforations consistent with contact with the hedgehog's spines. While apples appear to be the main fruits taken in this way, others, such as pears, strawberries, grapes and plums, are also known to have been carried on the hedgehog's spiky back from time to time. Clearly, the urchin knows the trick of divesting itself of its fruity burden, once home.

What is still not clear from all this is whether food-gathering is the hedgehog's primary object in rolling on fruit. My personal belief is that it is not. A significant point here is that hedgehogs have been observed to roll on a variety of other objects, such as beetles and flowers, the latter especially so, it seems, if strongly scented. To my mind, this immediately suggests a quite different motive – an attempt, probably, to control the parasites (principally fleas and ticks) with which these endearing little mammals are commonly heavily infested or perhaps alleviate the irritation they cause. Since apples (particularly crabs), pears, strawberries, and other fruits, are all highly acidic, and many beetles exude irritant substances for defensive purposes, it could well be that the hedgehog rolls on and spikes them in an attempt to use their juices as its own patent insecticide. Anything highly scented, like the flowers, might be instinctively thought of as equally useful and so treated in the same way.

There can be little doubt, I think, that the hedgehog's fleas must, at times, be a considerable trial to it, which could very well explain another of their behavioural traits. Unusually for mammals, hedgehogs enjoy a bath and may go to some lengths to satisfy their apparent desire for freshness, even in the coldest weather when they ought to be hibernating. One lady, awakened by the noise of a burst overflow pipe, went outside to find a truly spartan hedgehog enjoying a shower bath from it, rolling and shaking itself as if intent on gaining the fullest possible benefit from the icy liquid. Since it was midwinter and freezing hard at the time, one is compelled to wonder if the animal was less of a masochist than first appears but was desperately seeking a means of quieting its parasites, which had become so troublesome as to disrupt its winter sleep!

9·MYTH TO REALITY?

ROC

It is one of the fascinations of those beasts of ancient myth that, while the majority are clearly quite fabulous and could never really have existed, some may well conceal a small element of fact which has been grossly exaggerated and overlaid with fanciful detail for narrative effect. The *roc* (Arabic *rukh*), or 'Elephant bird', would seem to be a prime example of the possibility of truth turned into fiction. The best known account of it is to be found in *The Thousand and One Nights*, a compilation of ever popular fabulous tales, apparently first translated into Arabic about AD 850 from far older Persian origins. Here, during his second voyage, Sinbad the Sailor tells of encountering the bird on a remote island, many days after leaving the port of Basra and sailing down the Red Sea and (presumably) far out into the Indian Ocean. Having become separated from his companions, he is picked up by the roc and deposited in its rocky eyrie, next to its enormous egg, which Sinbad discovers to have a circumference of over fifty paces. Amazingly, he survives his terrific ordeal and even manages to escape by tying himself to the roc's leg. Indeed, it appears that it is really his small size which saves him, since this flying colossus was said to feed its young on elephants!

All pure fiction, of course: no bird could possibly attain such a monstrous size, much less take to the air. At the same time, giant birds *have* existed in the not-too-distant past, and one of them might very well fit the locale of Sinbad's ill-fated voyage. Had the intrepid seafarer's ship taken him SSW, an admittedly somewhat lengthy voyage might have brought him to the shores of the island of Madagascar (now the Malagasy Republic), where there were indeed at one time huge birds, considerably larger than any ostrich though like the latter flightless. Opinions differ as to when these great creatures became extinct, but it is clear that they lived on until well into historic times. Several species flourished amid the island's dense forests and swamps, but largest of them all was *Aepyornis maximus*: a real giant among birds, taller and heavier far than any ostrich (to which it was related), with a height of at least 10 ft (3 m) and a weight of around 990 lb (450 kg). Its eggs, too, were enormous, if not quite so large as those of Sinbad's roc: 15 in (38 cm) long, about 3 ft (90 cm) round, with the capacity of six ostrich eggs or 48 chickens' eggs. In the history of the world's birds, only the New Zealand moa or *Dinornis* has ever exceeded *Aepyornis* in size.

Could the *Aepyornis* have been the roc of legend, vastly aggrandised and turned into a bird of prey to make a more impressive tale? It seems possible, especially in view of its locale. Madagascar had certainly long been known to the early mediaeval Arabs, if only superficially, its remoteness and difficult terrain being sufficient to allow it to retain its mystery. Moreover, reports of huge birds in this strange, hostile, densely forested island had been current long before the 'Night' tales appeared. The fifth-century BC historian Herodotus tells of legends gained from Egyptian priests of great birds capable of carrying off men to be found somewhere in the region to the east of the mainland. Any chance sight of the eggs alone, whether *in situ* or offered for trade, might have prompted such tales, for they are large even for such a giant as *Aepyornis* – almost disproportionately so. After all, Persians, Arabs and Egyptians were familiar enough with the ostrich and the size of its eggs (c. 6 in – 15 cm), and if there were birds that could produce eggs several times that of this large species, they must surely be giants indeed!

Ironically, the *Aepyornis* itself was considered a myth by western zoologists until discovery of its bones and eggs, some of them containing half-developed chicks, perfectly preserved in the island's swamps and coastal sand dunes, left no room for doubt. Indeed, it seems to have only just escaped the doubtful privilege of becoming a zoo animal, since there is evidence to suggest that a few roc were still alive about 1867. The reasons for *Aepyornis maximus*' final demise are not entirely clear, but it seems probable that a combination of hunting and gradual forest clearance, forcing the birds into crocodile-infested regions, were among contributory factors.

PHOENIX

On the face of it, the phoenix seems just about the least likely of all mythological animals, and that is to say a good deal. After all, what possible factual basis can there be for a bird that was supposed to deliberately set itself on fire, and then become resurrected from its own ashes! Clearly, if there *is* any real natural history here it has become heavily overlaid and obscured by symbolism, closely linked to the phoenix' part in the Ancient Egyptians' worship of their sun-god, Amon-Ra. Writing about the customs and beliefs of the Egyptians in Book Two

127

of his monumental *Histories*, the Greek historian Herodotus tells us that this handsome, eagle-like bird, with its part-golden, part-red plumage, only appeared once every five hundred years, when it flew from Arabia to Egypt on the fiery death of its father, whose ashes it carried enveloped in myrrh and formed into the shape of an egg, the latter then placed in the Temple of the Sun at Heliopolis. Herodotus added that he did not believe the story, but simply related it as told to him. Others down the centuries have been considerably more credulous, more especially in mediaeval times.

If we disregard the overlay of fantasy, some clue to the origin of the phoenix and its fiery nativity can be gained by looking at it purely and simply as it is still portrayed in symbol and design today, for example in the emblems and trade marks of various fire insurance companies – that is, with its wings raised and rising out of a sea of flame. Is there, therefore, anything in bird behaviour which might possibly correspond to this? Unlikely as it seems, there is. For reasons that will be referred to later, some birds do seem to have a sort of propensity for fire and flame and, indeed, have occasionally been seen to behave like nothing short of feathered pyromaniacs. Rooks, for example, are known to take burning embers, twigs or even still burning cigarette stubs to their nests and, whether by accident or design, set fire to them and sometimes the trees themselves by such means. There are also historical references to this sort of thing happening with thatched buildings, notably in the Great Chronicle of London of 1203. That some birds seem quite fascinated by fire has been demonstrated in controlled experiments, notably by Dr Maurice Burton and his daughter Jane. The Burtons' tame rook, Niger, when presented with an ignited match, immediately thrust it under its wings, which it raised and flapped slightly to avoid burning, displaying at the same time every indication of enjoyment and even something akin to ecstasy. When its aviary straw was lit, the bird produced an even more phoenix-like response, standing over the naked flames with spread wings vibrating and head raised. Because of its constant movements, plus the fact that Niger was careful to lower the whitish, protective nicticating membrane, typical of most birds and many other animals, over its eyes, no injury was ever sustained from its dangerous 'playing with fire'.

Just how many species of birds engage in activity of this kind is undetermined. It can scarcely be part of their usual pattern of behaviour, although there must have been many who have watched common house sparrows perched on chimney tops and raising their wings to allow smoke to percolate their feathers. What does seem likely is that the birds' fire-and smoke-bathing is on a par with the avian phenomenon known as 'anting': a curious activity which involves the bird standing amidst a milling throng of ants and picking them up and placing or actually

The tusks – actually elongated incisor teeth – of the narwhal (**Monodon monoceros**) were in mediaeval and later times commonly passed off as unicorn horns, changing hands for large sums of money.

rubbing them into its flight feathers or down. Recorded from some 250 species of birds, anting quite probably affords the participants a certain stimulatory pleasure, although its main purpose would seem to be to control the activity and numbers of their itch-inducing feather-mites by means of the ants' formic acid. Presumably it is for much the same purpose that the more adventurous birds use fire and smoke, and one can easily visualize a situation where an early, impressionable observer might have used the sight of such activity to come up with a far more extreme, cosmic concept in the shape of the fabulous phoenix.

UNICORN

The unicorn of mediaeval romance and chivalry has exceedingly hazy origins. Its ennoblement to a handsome, usually white, horse-like creature, with a single spiral horn sprouting from the centre of its forehead would seem, in part, to be a refinement of earlier, only vaguely understood accounts of such creatures. Classical writers describe the unicorn as having a stag's head, the feet of an elephant, the tail of a bear, and the rest of the body like that of a horse. They go on to say that its single horn was black, and two cubits (3 ft or 1 m) long, and its cry a deep lowing noise. In fact, it is probable that descriptions of this sort really applied to the rhinoceros, known to the Greeks as *monoceros* and the Romans as *unicornis*, since the Asian version of this great mammal has indeed one, often very long horn, whereas its African counterpart has two.

Just how the unicorn became transformed into the elegant heraldic creature we know so well from a variety of old drawings, carvings and armorial bearings it is difficult to say, but one theory has it that its origins lie in the Arabian oryx (*Oryx leucoryx*), a beautiful antelope with two long, slightly backward-curved horns which might appear as one when considerable controversy until American zoologist Dr J.F. Gennaro discovered a method of definitely distinguishing octopus tissue from that of squid and other animals.

Whether the dread of the kraken that undoubtedly existed in the past was linked to actual attacks from it, we cannot really say. More recent retaliatory responses from giant squid are on record (page 97), although

The fact that few Europeans could claim to have actually seen a unicorn in its imagined guise naturally increased its mystique, and its horn, in particular, was much sought after, since it was supposed to have miraculous healing powers and might also provide a protection against deadly poisons. Thus, any unfamiliar animal horn that looked as if it might have come from a unicorn could often be passed off as such and sold at considerable profit. One so-called unicorn-horn, seen at Windsor in 1598, was valued at £10,000 – a vast sum in those days. Said to have been found in 1577 on an island in Frobisher's Strait (Bay), North Canada, the horn is described as being about 8½ spans, or 76 inches (193 cm), which almost certainly identifies it as that of the narwhal or 'sea unicorn' (*Monodon monoceros*), although this cetacean's horn is actually an enormously elongated incisor tooth or tusk, of spiral structure, which can attain a length of 8 feet (2.4 m). Only the male narwhal displays the tusk, but occasional individuals sport two, which must have given those venturesome Icelandic Norsemen who hunted narwhal in the early Middle Ages considerable joy, since they are said to have done particularly well out of the 'unicorn horn' business.

KRAKEN

The kraken, according to legend, is an immense sea-monster, Norwegian in origin, whose described characters somehow seem very much in keeping with that country's rather mysterious, steep-sided fjords and awe-inspiring maelstrom or giant whirlpool. Many of its supposed appearances were no less alarming for being subtle: what sailors and fishermen took for vast islands would suddenly loom out of the mist, and might even be landed upon, but then as soon as camp was made and fires lit on its back the monster submerged, taking the men with it. Not infrequently, the size of these living islands was given as more than a mile! Dreadful nonsense, of course, yet there is some evidence that the kraken, in its less exaggerated guise and more revealing moments, might not have been entirely mythical but had as its basis some very large denizen of the seas. Bishop Erik Pontoppidan describes the kraken in his *Natural History of Norway* (1752) as having a round, flat body, provided with a large number of arms or branches, adding that it is undoubtedly the largest sea-monster in the world. Today most accept this as an indication that the kraken of legend was either a giant octopus or squid. Smaller squid must have been familiar to and frequently caught by Norse fishermen, but there are certain much less forthcoming species (*Architeuthis*) which can attain a truly enormous size; in fact, no-one really knows just how big they might grow, since they tend to be rather retiring and shy, spending most of their time at great depths. Of the few specimens that have actually come to light, the largest was some 57 feet (17 m) from tail to tentacle-tip, and while exaggeration clearly plays a part in those others seen at sea there are almost certainly very much larger squid placidly and for the most part inoffensively roaming the oceans of the world. Giant octopus are equally possible candidates for the identity of the kraken. Until recently these even more publicity-shunning cephalopod molluscs were thought to attain only modest size, but there is now evidence to indicate that one species, called *Octopus giganteus verilli*, may occasionally attain a size of 200 ft (60 m) across: that is, from tentacle-tip to tentacle-tip. The assumption is based on a single specimen discovered washed up on the beach at St Augustine, Florida, as long ago as 1896. The carcase was so mutilated and lacking in tentacles and other identifying features that it was the subject of considerable controversy until American zoologist Dr J.F. Gennare discovered a method of definitely distinguishing octopus tissue from that of squid and other animals.

Whether the dread of the kraken that undoubtedly existed in the past was linked to actual attacks from it, we cannot really say. More recent retaliatory responses from giant squid are on record (page 97), although they can scarcely be considered everyday occurrences. Whether giant octopus might prove equally irritable and indiscriminatory with regard to man and his ships, perhaps simply because of their size, again, no-one really knows. Perhaps fear of the kraken was simply that unformulated horror of the unknown or half-known which many people still have of the ocean depths and deep waters generally.

DRAGONS

Trying to identify the dragon of myth and legend is a virtually impossible task, since it took so many forms, in different cultures and at different times. In its various guises, it appears in the mythologies of Greece, Rome and other parts of Europe, in Africa, the Near East, in China and Japan, in pre-Columbian America, and even in the Pacific Islands such as Hawaii. Later, of course, it became an essential feature in tales of European chivalry and derring-do. Many of these fearsome beasts were clearly composites, made up of various known animals. Thus, a typical Classical or European dragon might have a scaly, snake-like body, clawed feet like those of a lion, bat's or eagle's wings, a horned head with red eyes, and a mouth that belched forth flame. Others were more clearly serpentine, lacking legs and wings, but with certain embellishments like frills and beard. In between and beyond they enjoyed, like Cleopatra, near infinite variety.

The basically serpentine or worm-like appearance of many dragons is not without significance, since the word dragon derives from the Greek *drakon* (Latin *draco*), meaning a serpent or great worm, and many early classical references to dragons almost certainly refer to giant snakes, reported as occurring in distant lands. In his *Natural History*, Pliny mentions dragons, 30–40 ft (9–12 m) long, in India: surely the Indian python. In the Bible, too, the dragon was the serpent of evil expelled from Heaven by the Archangel Michael, which doubtless explains why the mythical beasts had ever after to be sought out and killed as a simple matter of duty by knights errant and local heroes, especially since the dragons made a habit of slaughtering everyone in sight and carrying off fair damsels to boot! Clearly fabulous though they are, such encounters or dragon presence are preserved in various European place-names. Drakelow ('dragon's burrow') and Wormley ('place of the great serpent') are two such in England, while the German towns of Drachenfels and Worms (where, it is said, Siegfried slew his 'great worm') are among others with similar associations.

As mentioned earlier, the dragon in its most typical form tended to be derived from a variety of animals, each of which had some feature particularly suggestive of strength or terror: eagle's wings, lion's claws and the tough, scaly body of a huge reptile. It is also not unlikely that some of them had as their basis transformations and distortions of reports of living beasts brought back by venturesome travellers. Some of these animals might have been terrestrial, others aquatic, the latter inclining towards the realm of the so-called sea serpent (see below). Crocodiles and monitor lizards might have been particularly suitable subjects for the storyteller to work on, during times when these reptiles were rarely seen out of Africa, just as the Komodo 'dragon' of Indonesia provided material for at least some aspects of dragon lore in China and Japan (where, incidentally, the dragon was considered a power for both good and evil). The Komodo dragon (*Varanus komodoensis*) grows to a length of 10 ft (3 m) and fulfils all the basic requirements for the mythical beast, except for its lack of wings; it also tends to be rather aggressive and is not above snatching at the nearest leg. There are flying lizards, too, which might well have added something to any final amalgam, though they are by no means large and their flight is little more than gliding, effected by frills of ribbed skin along the sides of the body. Modern science, perhaps half tongue-in-cheek, affords these would-be aeronauts of the lizard world the generic name of *Draco*.

One rather intriguing behavioural aspect of lizards, large and small, lies in their habit of constantly flicking their forked tongues in and out to test the air. Could this characteristic have originated the mythical dragon's fire-breathing aspects? To the more fancifully inclined, doubtless observing from a respectful distance, the rapidity of the tongue's movements, together with its thinness, flexibility and often flame-red colour, might very easily have prompted such an impression.

SEA SERPENTS

It is one of the obscurities and charms of the English language that 'sea snake' and 'sea serpent', while virtual synonyms, tend to refer to very different beasts. Sea snakes (family Hydrophidae) are a zoological fact, whereas sea serpents are, as yet, nothing of the kind. What is more, the former fall rather short of according to the picture of the great sea serpent of myth and legend, amplified by countless observers throughout history until almost the present day. For one thing, there is the great disparity of size. In sea serpents, this can apparently range, according to observer and the type of creature 'seen', from about 20 to as much as 100 ft (6–30 m), or more, whereas sea snakes rarely attain a length of 10 ft (3 m) and are more usually about half that. The Hydrophidae do, admittedly, spend a good deal of their time at or near the surface of the sea, but their locomotion there is effected by lateral convolutions, not vertical, such as would seem to be one of the typical characteristics of sea serpents. Another point is that whereas sea serpents of one kind or another have allegedly been observed in virtually every part of the world, sea snakes are confined to tropical oceans.

If sea serpents are not true snakes, then what are they? Are they existing animals that have been consistently misinterpreted, unknown species, surviving aquatic dinosaurs, or what? The question has puzzled naturalists for centuries, not least because the sea serpents seem to occur in a variety of forms. However, a number of theories have been postulated to account for at least some of those types with recurrently described features, which it will be as well to relate first. In many cases all that is seen is a long, relatively thin, perhaps slightly tapering neck, bearing a horse-like, sheep-like, or perhaps cat-like face, protruding several feet from the water, typically at an angle of some 30–45 degrees; when the body is seen, it is commonly described as humped, with sometimes as many as ten such protuberances showing above the water line. Eyes, when seen, can be either large and staring or small and inconspicuous, and sometimes there are small horns or ear-like projections on the head. Some observers tell of a sort of mane or dorsal fin running down part of the back. Nearly all insist that when humps are seen they are clearly part of the same animal, which ought to dispose of any suggestion that we might be dealing with a school of otters, porpoises, dolphins or other cetaceans: these, in any case, would scarcely remain in position long enough to account for such frequently observed phenomena. In some cases, the head is so small, indistinct and apparently undifferentiated from the body as to present a particularly serpent-like appearance, were it not for the fact that this type, like nearly all the others, tends to progress by means of vertical undulations: a physical impossibility in any reptile or fish, including the oar-fish, which has not infrequently been offered as a possible identity of many a sea serpent.

Some crypto-zoologists, in trying to explain such observations in terms of known animal species, are convinced the subjects are mammalian – not the 'schools' mentioned earlier but one particular species, the leopard seal (*Hydrurga leptonyx*). The latter certainly presents at least some of the characteristics described of sea serpents, if not their size, although this, as we have seen, is commonly a subject of exaggeration with respect to many *known* animal groups. Firstly, there is the seal's method of swimming, which is by alternate plunges and surfacings, propelled by fore-flippers and tail: in effect, not unlike a human swimmer doing the butterfly-stroke, though infinitely more graceful. The large head is supported by a 3–4 ft (90–120 cm) neck, which is commonly held above water when the animal is cruising about and looking for potential prey, such as other seal species, penguins and fish. Even the leopard seal's limited overall length – about 10–12 ft (3–3.6 m) – might not disqualify it as the basis of the sea serpent most commonly described, since the implication in many reports is that the greater part of the latter's body is hidden beneath the waves. One real difficulty with the identification, though, lies in the sea serpent's consistently observed humps. A leopard seal might display one or two – the top of its curved back and tail – but scarcely a series of them. Another is that *leptonyx* is more or less confined to the Antarctic region, only occasionally venturing north to the southern seas of Australia, Africa and South America. It has, however, been suggested that there could be other species of leopard seals occurring in northern seas, perhaps even one with an unusually long neck, such as would fit the description of sea serpents rather more closely. Hitherto unconfirmed reports from Arctic Eskimos indicate that such an animal could well exist in that region.

Another group of mammals that might be linked to at least some of the sea serpents' reported features, and would at least fulfil the requirement of size, are, of course, whales. We may protest that whales would surely be familiar to those experienced seamen, fishermen and the like from whom so many sea serpent reports derive, but the fact is there are many whale species whose appearance and habits are very little known and which have never or scarcely ever been caught. Among these, it is just possible that there is still existing some latter-day relative of the presumed extinct zeuglodonts (*Basiliosaurus*), which crypto-zoologist Dr Roy Mackal is inclined to link with the Canadian lake monster known as the Ogopogo (page 147). There is, according to Mackal, much to be said in favour of postulating this identity for those sea serpents allegedly seen for many years off Vancouver Island, British Columbia, where fossils of these great shark-like 'sea dragons' have been found. Zeuglodonts apparently roamed almost throughout the world's oceans until as recently, palaeontologically speaking, as 25 million years ago, and if some do still exist they would fit almost all the physical requirements of the classic sea serpent – with large, tooth-filled head, short fore flippers and largely undifferentiated body attaining lengths of up to 70 ft (21 m). Being mammals, they would also be likely to swim in the approved 'serpentine' manner, or something approximating to it, at least.

Intriguingly, there are even some invertebrate animals that might be linked to the sea serpent saga, among them giant squids and octopus, whose massive body and tentacles occasionally appearing above water might have prompted at least some reports. If this seems a little unlikely, others are perhaps rather more plausible candidates. One suggestion has it that immense colonies of larval tunicates could provide the answer to our zoological enigma. These curious marine animals, which zoologists consider may form a halfway stage of evolution between invertebrate and vertebrate (notably in the possession of a backbone and notochord in the larva only), are colonial as larvae, joining together as one communal animal to form lengths of over 30 ft (9 m), by perhaps a foot across. In some sexual forms, with young animals budding off but still attached to the parents, such chains have been known to attain nearly three times that length. This, combined with the fact that such colonies actually progress by vertical undulations, puts them well into the sea serpent category. Since there is often considerable uniformity of thickness and shape, some tunicate colonies are truly snake-like in appearance. In others, the effect is more tapering, with one end closed and the other having an eye-like opening: the whole effect being like that of a giant one-eyed tadpole which, it may be significant to mention, has been reported as another form of sea serpent.

Finally, it must be added that many sea serpent sightings have almost certainly been straightforward misinterpretations of quite ordinary, down-to-earth phenomena. As long ago as 1907, E. Kay Robinson tells in the magazine *Country-Side* of seeing what he felt sure, at the outset, was a sea serpent whilst looking out to sea. It appeared, he said, to be moving along at a considerable speed, just as sea serpents are commonly said to do, and looked exactly like the beast of legend, with parts of its body showing as humps above the water at regular intervals. Robinson then focussed a powerful telescope upon the 'creature' – which immediately proved to be no more than a procession of compact flocks of small black sea-birds skimming one behind the other over the surface of the sea. With the use of binoculars only, the writer adds, the birds had been a sea serpent *par excellence* and anyone without visual aid would quite probably have accepted them as such. Clearly, one does not wish to imply from this that every sea serpent observation can be dismissed in a similar way. However, it does perhaps suggest that if one is predisposed to their existence they are perhaps more likely to be 'seen' than if one is completely objective about such things.

GIANTS, DWARFS AND BEAST-MEN

Giants and their kin bestride the mythology, folklore and fairy tales of almost every land. Especially typical of Ancient Greek, Teutonic and Celtic peoples, many of them form an essential part of creation myths and were not unnaturally capable of performing titanic deeds, like the Titans themselves (the twelve sons of Uranus) and the Irish Fingal, who single-handedly constructed the Giant's Causeway off the north coast of Ireland. In more down-to-earth situations, they made suitably formidable opponents for would-be heroes, while the mere mention of giants and man-eating ogres must in earlier times have been sufficient to bring recalcitrant children to heel and send them off to bed with many a subsequent nightmare.

Many giants were clearly figurative. Since they were mostly evil, or at least threatening and powerful, it was only natural that they should be large, reflecting the magnitude of the task to be overcome or maybe with

136

certain non-human attributes, such as the possession of but a single eye, set in the centre of their foreheads, like the Cyclops encountered by Odysseus and his men. Needless to say, they cannot really have lived: at least, not in their most extreme forms. Very tall men have existed, and still do, but their eminence is rarely, if ever, matched by corresponding strength and musculature. A few human races still flourishing today are unusually tall – the Watusi herdsmen of Central Africa average well over 6 ft (1.8 m), with the occasional individual more than 7 ft (2.1 m) – but they are uncommon, and most other giants are physical freaks. Almost invariably, they suffer from certain debilitating conditions, resulting from over-activity of the pituitary gland, which brings with it distorted vision, even blindness, in addition to uneven enlargement of the bone structure. They also tend to be short-lived, rarely exceeding forty years, weakly, ungainly and, often, intellectually dull – features which both contradict and support the mythical giant image. In myth and fable, giants may be described as fierce and strong, yet they are nearly always easily outwitted by their more cunning human adversary, and indeed are often depicted as rather stupid.

That tradition and folklore loves big men is indicated by the fact that even those giants who played no part in mythology – actual historical or apocryphal figures like Og, King of Bashan and Gilead or Chang, the Chinese giant – could rely upon having several feet added to their height by repute, as might any large fellow who had the misfortune to be 'managed' by showmen or fair-people. The largest properly authenticated giant known to have lived, apparently, was an American, Robert Pershing Wardlow (1918–40), who was 8 ft 11 in (2.7 m) and weighed 31 stone 5 lb (199 kg) at his death. A number of others (English, American, German, Portuguese, Finnish, Egyptian, Libyan) have also exceeded 8 ft (2.4 m) and a good many others are recorded at around 7 ft 7 in (2.3 m), but all are comparative rarities and no advertisement for the giant of myth. The fact is that human physiology works best between certain size limits – about 5–6 ft (1.5–1.8 m), with the optimum inclining towards the lower end of the scale. Today, the world average height for *Homo sapiens* is, in fact, 5 ft 5 in (1.7 m).

Innocuous and inoffensive as they must have been, it is, of course, likely that the occasional very tall men – and women – who existed in past times contributed at least something to the giant of myth, suitably exaggerated for effect. One can even imagine situations where, like the Biblical Goliath, such an overgrown individual might actually have been used by army generals to inspire terror in the opposing ranks, merely through his appearance, although it is doubtful if the poor fellow (doubtless weighed down by his armour) would have proved much of a soldier. It is a curious fact, indeed, that most big men tend to be 'gentle giants', so it is quite probable that our armed titan's heart might not have been in the business in the first place.

It is perhaps not without significance that those 'little people' at the other end of the human size scale – the dwarfs, elves, fairies – are often pictured in traditional myth and fairy lore as mischievous and malevolent. If you lacked stature and strength, you made up for it in other more subtle ways, perhaps by simply exerting your authority or by switching new-born babes for considerably less prepossessing gnomish nurslings. Parents mortified to find that their son and heir 'grew up' to be a dwarf might, perhaps, have been excused for believing that he had been swapped in the cradle by these naturally diminutive beings. Arrived at maturity, it seems probable that many of these unfortunates remained single and died celibate, for fear that they might breed a generation of little folk, although such notions would have been quite unfounded since dwarfism is not hereditary but the result of arrested infantile growth. True dwarfs are quite capable of siring perfectly normal offspring, as of course are those few *races* that rarely grow beyond about 4½ ft (1.4 m), such as the Ituri pygmies of Central Africa, some Andaman Islanders, and others whose existence is less fully substantiated.

Mythology is equally replete with other near-humans, such as the classical anthropophagi (literally 'man-eaters'), which might have had their origins in cannibal peoples or those whose custom it was to consume the bodies of their recently departed relatives in order to perpetuate their merits. Still more may have been based on early, ignorant sightings of monkeys and apes or perhaps of strange rituals involving men wearing the skins of animals. Such, for example, might have prompted creation of the satyrs: forest gods especially associated with fertility and the rites that went with it. They varied in form, some being human-like except for small goat-like horns and ears, and goatish legs, others with monkey- or baboon-like faces and tails. All were generally lecherous in the extreme: an attribute that has long been linked to monkeys, apes and goats. Falstaff describes Justice Shallow as being 'lecherous as a monkey' in Shakespeare's *Henry IV*, Part 2.

Some beast-men, like the Greek centaurs, with the head and trunk of a man but the legs and body of a horse, appear wholly fanciful, with no conceivable foundation in fact. It has, however, been suggested that one possible origin for these often wise and learned beings (one of whom, Chiron, was the tutor of a number of classical heroes) had their origin in the fearful imaginings of those primitive tribes who lacked and had never seen horses and thus mistook horsemen for composite creatures. Both the Incas of Peru and the Aztecs of Mexico are said to have been terrified by their first sight of mounted Spaniards.

The best-known aquatic beast-men of myth, legend and folklore are, of course, the mer-people, closely linked to a whole range of similar beings, such as the fish-tailed god of the oceans, Poseidon (Neptune to the Romans), the Tritons, fish-maiden attendants on Aphrodite, the Nereids and Sirens (sea-nymphs), Dagon, sea-god of the Babylonians, and many more from a whole range of civilisations. All were typically human to the waist and fish below. Mermaids and Sirens, in particular, had sweet voices which, together with their beauteous upper parts, might lure unwary sailors to their doom. In some cases, humans might actually be enticed to live beneath the waves or the reverse take place – mermaids (or mermen) electing to live on land with their chosen bipedal mates. Belief in such beings dies hard and sailors, fishermen and sea-travellers down the centuries have relayed many a sighting of mermaids, perhaps seated on some convenient rock, combing their hair or cradling a child in their arms (see below). Clearly, if you were already convinced of mermaids' existence you saw them more readily. Thus, when Columbus reported seeing three mermaids lift their heads out of the water off the island of Haiti in 1493 he was privileged only in the scientific sense, in that he was probably the first westerner to observe the New World manatee (*Trichecus manatus*). He would not have been aware of the fact, of course, and indeed the explorer's reaction seems merely to have been disappointment that his 'mermaids' were less beautiful than he had been led to suppose. The manatees of Central and South America and West Africa, as well as the dugong (*Dugong dugon*), which ranges from East Africa, through the Middle East to India and the Western Pacific, have often been postulated as one of the probable origins of the mermaid myth because of their possession of certain vaguely human attributes. The transformation would, however, require the eye of faith and a considerable pre-disposition towards mermaid existence, since the animal's head and upper parts are scarcely those of even the most hideously featured man or woman. Such minor details might nevertheless have been balanced by their habit of standing on their hind flippers half out of water, together with the females' vaguely human-like breasts and their occasional cradling of the single pup in one fore-flipper, much as a woman might nurse her baby. Modern taxonomists, clearly well up with their classical mythology, classify the manatees and dugong as Sirenia, although unfortunately these marine mammals do not seem to possess the melodious voice of their semi-human namesakes, such as might add the finishing touch to their championing as real-life mermaids. That deficiency might very easily have been made up, however, by the ancients' tendency to amalgamate the features of different animals: in this case, perhaps, seals, whose wailing cries (like those of cats) are often remarkably human, and especially impressive on the imagination when heard at night.

FABLE AND FACT

Animals have been known to be born with two heads, as well as extra limbs, but they are biological freaks and the former, in particular, do not generally live long. Thus, mythological beasts like the amphisbaena, with a head at each end of its body, and the hydra, with nine borne at the end of writhing tentacles, are total impossibilities and, if based on any sort of fact at all, clearly arise from a combination of misobservation and fertile imagination. The amphisbaena, whose name derives from the Greek meaning 'going both ways', was believed by classical and mediaeval naturalists to be serpentine in form, with dragon's wings, at which point it diverges somewhat from the existing amphisbaenas, a little-known group of legless lizards still to be found in southern Europe, the Middle East, Africa and parts of the Americas. With a length that varies between 1 and 2 ft (30–60 cm), the zoologist's amphisbaena is not unlike the European slow-worm in general appearance, with its head so little differentiated from its body, and exceedingly minute eyes, as to make it look as if it really does not know whether it is coming or going. Early natural historians must surely have seen these curious lizards from time to time, but whether they formed the basis of their own particular two-headed beast is unclear. They could certainly not have seen anything very much like the fearsome hydra, slain with difficulty by Hercules during one of his 'labours', although its imaginative form may owe something to the octopus or squid. Today, the hydra lives on only in the form of a much less awe-inspiring animal: a tiny freshwater coelenterate, related to the jellyfish, whose sole resemblance to its fabulous counterpart lies in the possession of up to a dozen or so thin waving tentacles for stinging and capturing its prey. Near-bathos of this sort has proved to be the fate of a good many mythical monsters!

Several classical snakes have 'survived' to find their way into modern zoology. The original python was a huge snake killed by the youthful Apollo, and it is clear that the Ancient Greeks knew something of these great constrictors, since one of their legends (immortalised in a famous statue in the Vatican) tells how Laocoon and his two sons were crushed to death by a pair of them. The asp, however, signals another departure into sheer fantasy, since in its purely mythological guise, as distinct from its association with Cleopatra (page 40), it bore wings, such as no real snake does; it was also in the habit of putting one ear to the ground and stuffing its tail in the other, and was thus the 'deaf adder' of the Bible (Psalm LVIII), which provides an interesting tie-in with snakes' actual auditory powers (page 39). Existing asps belong to the viper group and have a Mediterranean distribution.

The salamander is another mythical beast that actually exists, in different but intriguingly connected form. Originally it was a winged, bipedal dragon, with a tail that is depicted as being tied in a knot. It was supposed to live in fire and was thus by way of being a good beast, since only the pure can survive the burning flames of hell. Classical writers like Aristotle and Pliny maintained that a salamander could actually quench fire merely by walking through it, on account of its exceptional coldness. It was also said to exude a milky poison from its mouth and be capable not merely of poisoning other animals but of infecting any fruit and water with which it came in contact. Existing salamanders are, like their close relatives the newts, cold and moist to the touch; they have poison-bearing tubercles in the skin, although the poison is innocuous enough where man is concerned; and one species, the European fire salamander (*Salamandra salamandra*), has bright lemon yellow areas on its glossy black skin, which the fancifully inclined might find it easy to link with a fire-living existence. It has further been suggested that since salamanders commonly hibernate in old logs, they might occasionally have been seen to emerge when one was placed on a fire, thus adding fuel, as it were, to the flame-living myth. Clearly, the fabulous salamander owed something, at least, to the real thing.

As we have seen, many mythical entities present, like the afore-mentioned hydra, a stark contrast with their identically named, living counterparts. Today's basilisk is an inoffensive lizard but the original possessor of its name was truly something to be avoided at all costs, since it was able to kill at a mere glance. Later, it seems, the basilisk became identified with the cockatrice, a name which the mediaeval French applied to the crocodile (*caucatrice*, from the Low Latin *cocodrillus*). Snake-locked Medusa, one of the three Gorgon sisters, enjoyed the power of turning anyone who looked at her into stone. To my mind, that fearsome female's name could not be better perpetuated than in the little snakelocks sea anemone (*Anemonia sulcata*), whose typically grey-green tentacles are highly suggestive of a head of writhing snakes. Sadly, zoology lets us down for once and applies the term Medusae to the free-swimming forms of coelenterates, such as jellyfish.

10·THE SEARCH FOR LIVING MONSTERS

DO THEY EXIST?

With all the rich variety of animal life that exists on Earth, enough to satisfy whole teams of zoologists working day and night for many generations to come, one would have thought there was no longer any need to people our world with large, unclassifiable beasts of the 'monster' type, such as our forbears were wont to do. The old Greek, Roman and mediaeval naturalists might have had some excuse for their credulity since it was only exceedingly slowly that even the position of the great land masses became known and explored, and new animals kept turning up all the time or were known only by rumour. But is it really feasible to suggest that today, with all the sophisticated methods of travel and detection we have available to us, there are huge reptiles or mammals of quite unknown species still to be found? Surely their very size would have brought them to our attention long before now? New species of animals *are* continually being found, but they are generally small and scarcely likely to be such as to hit the popular newspaper headlines.

If he is a sensible man, the zoologist is non-committal in the matter; he is sceptical, of course, but at the same time open-minded as to the possibility of such things, at least. The fact is that there are still plenty of areas in the world where almost anything could turn up. The swampy jungles of the Congo River basin, in Africa, and that vast region of the Upper Amazon and the Rio Negro, where the political borders of the South American states of Brazil, Colombia and Venezuela meet are still almost totally uncharted, zoologically speaking. Large areas of Central Asia and the great wastelands of Siberia are almost equally little known. A combination of difficult terrain and inhospitable climate tend to make such areas, comprising many thousands of square miles, only accessible to and habitable by the animals and plants and those indigenous peoples who have become adapted to the pattern of living imposed upon them by nature. Who knows what unknown creatures these and similar terrains might harbour?

Of course, mere rumour will hardly do. Nor is first-hand observation invariably assured of doing much better, since to be disbelieved has always tended to be the lot of even the most eminent intrepid explorers bringing back news of strange, new species from unknown parts. The animals concerned do not have to be all that outlandish, either. The okapi, that strange giraffe-relative which looks rather like a cross between a horse and an antelope, was certainly regarded with considerable scepticism until Sir Harry Johnston finally removed all doubts of its existence in the Congo in 1900. Even specimens tend to be regarded with a measure of suspicion, at least partly because animal fakers have done their best to keep zoologists confused and guessing right down the ages. When the first specimen of the Australian platypus found its way to the British Natural History Museum, it was totally rejected. After all, what could one say of a mammal with a duck's bill and webbed feet, and one moreover that was said to lay eggs. An elaborate mock-up, surely!

Entrenchments of doubt are likely to be even more difficult to surmount when reports concern the alleged continued existence of animals hitherto known only as fossils, even though a number of such discoveries have actually been made in recent years. The classic example of a so-called 'living fossil' is, of course, the coelacanth, an archaic fish long thought by ichthyologists and palaeontologists to have become extinct some 70 million years ago, until a living one was caught off Madagascar in 1938. Perhaps we should not be too sceptical about even more spectactular survivals, for there are other groups with equally and sometimes far more venerable pedigrees, like the horseshoe 'crabs' – actually more closely related to spiders – which have come down to us virtually unchanged from Cambrian times, some 550 million years ago. With depths that are, in parts (the Marianas Trench in the western Pacific), greater than the height of Mount Everest, the world's oceans are almost certain to yield many surprises in the future, in so far as we shall ever be able to explore them properly. Such new species as do turn up from this source are often obtained by accident, like the hitherto completely unknown species of 'megamouth' shark, 15 ft (4.5 m) long, dredged up by a United States Navy ship in 1976.

Some postulated survivals from prehistoric times make one catch one's breath with excitement – or disbelief. Surely, they cannot really be true? In 1974, members of an English expedition to Kenya caught glimpses of a strange bat-like creature many feet across the wings which bore every resemblance to a pterodactyl. Another was seen in Namibia the following year. Neither seems to have been a bat, since its teeth were observed by an earlier traveller to be of uniform size, whereas a bat's are typically mammalian, differentiated into canines, incisors and molars. If the creature *was* a pterodactyl, then any future expedition in search of it will need to bring back a living specimen, just as Professor Challenger of *The Lost World* found it necessary to do in order to finally confound his detractors.

LAKE MONSTERS

Scotland's Loch Ness is one of the most famous stretches of inland water in the world. Forming part of the geological fault that almost completely bisects the Scottish Highlands, it stretches 21¾ miles (35 km) from Inverness on the north-east coast to Fort William in the south-west, where it is linked by the Caledonian Canal to Lochs Oich, Lochy and Linnhe, the last-mentioned emptying into the Atlantic Ocean. It is probably fair to say that the loch is not particularly appealing in itself, except of course to local residents; indeed, its aspect is commonly gloomy and severe, increased by the steep, brooding cliffs that surround it; yet every year it attracts visitors from all over the world, most of whom come in the hope of catching a glimpse of its most famous resident, the Loch Ness Monster, popularly shortened to 'Nessie'. The fact that the beast, if it exists at all, has never yet been identified forms no obstacle to their enthusiasm; in fact, it is probable that they would not come if Nessie were no longer a mystery.

Whatever one may say about the likelihood of some strange, unknown beast lurking in the murky depths of the loch (and its waters *are* deep: 750 and possibly as much as 900 ft, 230–275 m, in parts), belief in it is of considerable antiquity and has not abated despite the scepticism with which it is regarded in most scientific circles. The first recorded 'observation' apparently dates back to AD 565 when St Columba, the bringer of Christianity to Scotland, is said to have seen Nessie from the loch's shore and forbidden it to molest a human swimmer. Sightings since then have run into thousands, many of them by highly reputable and unimaginative people, including the monks of the Benedictine Abbey which overlooks the loch at Fort Augustus. Until quite recently, fishermen were wary of venturing far out into the loch and children were warned not to play near its shores, since the beast has the reputation of being amphibious. Latterly, Nessie has been photographed, filmed, taped and its underwater presence recorded by sonar. It has even been afforded a scientific name, *Nessiteras rhombopteryx*, by Sir Peter Scott, one of the monster's firmest supporters: rather unwarrantably, since, despite all the mass of half-evidence (and it is perhaps even less than that), the creature's phylogenetic affinities remain obscure, to say the least.

Zoologists have a perfect right to be sceptical, for the plain fact is that, as in so many other elusive present-day unknown but widely postulated beasts, not a shred of *physical* evidence has ever come to light from St Columba's date right down to the present: no skulls or bones or skin fragments; not even any authenticated foot (or flipper) prints, although the beasts have, it seems, been known to come ashore and have even been seen crossing roads near the loch – one, it is alleged, carrying a sheep in its mouth! Nessie-adherents not unnaturally shrug such objections aside. They point to the fact that since the creature is principally aquatic, it would be likely to die in the loch, so that any remains of former generations would be lost in the virtually inaccessible mud at the loch's bottom. To support their argument, they add that the bodies of human swimmers occasionally drowned in the loch are rarely cast ashore, at least partly because of the loch's variable underwater currents which suck them down. First-hand observations of Nessie also conform to a remarkably similar pattern, most of them telling of a large creature, varying in length from about 15 to 60 ft (4.5–18 m), with a long, relatively slender neck, small rather reptilian head, on which there are sometimes small horns, and roundish, heavy body, commonly showing as two or more humps; occasionally glimpsed are a long, powerful, slightly blunt-ended tail and two pairs of broad, diamond-shaped flippers. Fishermen have told of its skin being rough and crinkly, rather like an elephant's; and several have reported it snorting and panting like a horse.

Recent underwater investigations, using special cameras and sonar equipment to register the presence of large moving bodies, have so far proved inconclusive, one problem being the difficulty of vision in the loch's depths, made darker by peat suspension. Muzzy underwater photographs taken by American Robert Rines in the 1970s of what might, given the eye of faith, be accepted as the monster itself, as well as one of its paddles, would seem to go some way towards confirming physical descriptions, providing support for arguments that the creature is probably a surviving plesiosaurus: a freshwater carnivorous dinosaur generally thought to have become extinct some 70 million years ago. If this is so, then it need never be short of food, since the loch is rich in shoals of fish of many kinds.

Much as one would like to believe in the Loch Ness Monster's existence, it has to be said that far more prosaic explanations can be offered for almost all of the more distant sightings of supposed monster presence and activity, and that includes some of the best photographs, such as the famous so-called Surgeon's Photograph, taken by gynaecologist Dr R.K. Wilson in 1934, which purports to show the monster's head and neck, and a more recent one of similar type taken in 1979 by Anthony Shiels. Both were taken at a considerable distance and neither is convincing. It is worth bearing in mind that distance and size of objects seen are often difficult to judge, even with binoculars or telescope, and as we have seen elsewhere people are rather prone to exaggerate the size and nature of animals they see or think they see. Thus it is possible to suggest all manner of living and non-living items to account for supposed monster sightings, and sceptical zoologists have not been slow to do so. Otters' tails, schools of otters, porpoises or seals (which, since they sometimes disport one behind the other, might account for the monster's humps), giant eels or the fins of killer whales, all and more have been offered as possible alternative explanations. (Porpoises, seals and whales are, of course, primarily marine or coastal but are known to make their way into inland waters from time to time.) Upturned boats, the wash caused by motor boats, or the boats themselves, rotting tree-trunks, gaseous matter arising from the loch's depths, even collective hallucination or auto-suggestion induced by past tradition or descriptions: the list of 'inorganic' alternatives seems equally endless. To Nessie-supporters it must often seem that the scientific establishment will suggest *anything* rather than believe.

Loch Ness may justly claim the most widely known and investigated lake monster, but it is far from unique in this respect. (Incidentally, when we speak of 'the monster' we must really mean several, since it could scarcely survive on its own, unless it were an animal Methuselah and a confirmed bachelor!) It, he or she has many brethren in other parts of the world, including some on its own doorstep, as it were. A whole string of Scottish lochs lay claim to their own monsters, kelpies or water-horses, including 'Morag' of Loch Morar, which is even deeper than Loch Ness. There are also reputed to be similar creatures in some of Ireland's loughs, while others have been reported from Russia, Iceland, Norway, Sweden, Patagonia (Argentina), Canada and the USA.

Russian 'Nessies' seem principally confined to Siberia, including Lakes Vorota, Labynkyr (whose 'dragon-like beast' is said to have on one occasion swallowed a hunter's dog), and Lake Khaiyr. The last-mentioned is of particular interest to the writer since when a report of one such sighting there appeared in Russian newspapers in 1964 I went to the length of writing to Professor A.M. Ryabchikov, Dean of Moscow University's Faculty of Geography, the department which had organised the relevant bio-geological expedition to the lake, asking for further details. Predictably, perhaps, he dismissed the alleged sighting as a 'misunderstanding', adding that there was not the slightest evidence for such a creature in the lake. It is, nevertheless, worth describing the alleged observation, since it is so clear-cut and definite, providing on the one hand what would seem to be direct evidence for such beasts' existence or, looked at another way, bearing all the hall-marks of an

Gladkikh's sketch of the Russian lake monster allegedly seen at Lake Khaiyr, Siberia, in 1964.

elaborate hoax. Briefly, what happened (or so it is alleged) was this. A man by the name of Gladkikh had gone down to the lake's edge to collect water, when he saw, he says, the creature creeping slowly out onto the shore. He does not, I think, mention how far away he was, but it was apparently close enough for him to describe the animal in some detail, notably in that it had a small somewhat reptilian head on a long, shiny neck, a huge body, blue-black in colour, with a vertically protruding fin. As he watched, Gladkikh went on, the creature inclined its head, giving the impression of nibbling the thin vegetation at the lake's edge. Then, it seems, panic set in and Gladkikh tells of running to fetch the expedition's chief biologist, but when they returned there was no sign of the beast, except for some traces of flattened grass and ripples on the lake's surface where the creature might have submerged. Later, we are told, several of the party, including the expedition's leader, saw the monster's head and fin appear from out of the middle of the lake; then it thrashed the water with its tail and disappeared.

As I have said, the whole episode does not seem to have been taken in the least bit seriously by the Russian scientific fraternity, though whether that is because of an entrenched scepticism, by no means confined to the USSR, or because they suspected a hoax, I cannot say. If it *was* a hoax, then the whole of the expedition seem to have been in on it!

Perhaps the only thing that can be said in support of such alleged sightings is that there often tends to be a tradition of monster presence among the local inhabitants – in Lake Khaiyr's case, the Yakuts. The same applies to Canada's most famous lake creature, the so-called Ogopogo which is said to lurk in Lake Okanagan, in British Columbia. Stone carvings or pteroglyphs on rocks near the lake, dating back to the seventeenth century, apparently depict the beast in stylised form and link with local legends that tell of a beast not above killing and swallowing horses, dogs and even men. Recent descriptions of the Ogopogo suggest that it displays certain differences from the Loch Ness and other monsters. It has, we are told, a tapering head, bearing visible teeth, a body that is armed with bony plates and a powerful *forked* tail. It is also said to swim fast (about 25 mph), with vertical undulations, occasionally 'blow' like a whale, and is scarcely ever seen ashore. Dr R.P. Mackal, an inveterate monster-hunter, takes such descriptions sufficiently seriously to suggest that the creature might be a surviving zeuglodont, or primitive whale of the family Basiliosauridae, a group generally considered to be long extinct (see page 136). Lake Okanagan's direct link with the Pacific Ocean renders this at least a *possibility*, both for the Ogopogo and for consistently described creatures said to have been seen in neighbouring lakes, as well as around Lake Winnipeg in central Canada, and right across to the opposite coast about the St Lawrence River. 'Ogopogo', it may be worth adding, is something of a joke name for Canada's answer to the Loch Ness Monster. It was apparently coined by a music hall artist in 1926 in response to several reported sightings at the time, and has no basis other than in the man's own inventiveness. The local Indian name for the beast is *Naitaka*, or variants thereof.

Across the border, in the United States of America, we find legends of other lake creatures, a proportion of which appear to bear at least some resemblance to both the Loch Ness and Lake Okanagan monsters, although that reported from the Valley River, in North Carolina, would seem to be of a very different character. Indian legends tell of something like a giant leech which has from time to time killed and consumed men, the bodies of others being found on the river bank with ears and nose eaten away. If it really does exist, which seems somewhat doubtful, there is little or nothing to link it with any known species.

Rather more serious scientific attention has latterly been paid to rumours of large, dinosaur-like creatures living in the rivers, lakes and swamps of the Central Congo River basin. Locals refer to these creatures by various names, among them *n'yamala* and *mokele-mbembe* and there is a considerable degree of consistency in their descriptions of them which emanate from a very wide area extending over the modern countries of southern Cameroon, eastern Gabon and the Congo Republic. With minor variations, pygmies and other natives of the region echo a tradition which dates back hundreds and perhaps thousands of years in telling of a creature elephantine in size, with heavy body, muscular tail, long neck and small head, on which there is usually a single large tooth or perhaps a horn. Living in caves in the banks of rivers and lakes, the beast is regarded with dread since it is said to attack canoes and kill the occupants, though apparently without eating them, its food consisting solely of vegetation, in pursuit of which it commonly comes ashore. It is also alleged to chase away hippopotami, possibly because the latter infringe its browsing rights!

Several scientific expeditions have been mounted to the Congo in recent years to try to obtain first-hand information about the *mokele-mbembe*, and reports so far suggest that there may indeed be some strange animal living there which does not accord with any known species. Whether it is a surviving sauropod, or dinosaur, as some believe, cannot yet be established with anything like certainty, but there have been tantalising glimpses which indicate at least the possibility of something of the kind. As recently as the early 1980s several Western observers told of seeing a 6–foot (2-m) long neck emerge from Lake Telle in the Likouala Region of the Congo and of witnessing the movement of some very large creature through the water accompanied by strange roars and growls. Unidentifiable tracks have been found, some with the suggestion of a heavy tail swinging from side to side. One of the great difficulties of establishing the truth of the matter lies in the terrain's inaccessibility and inhospitable nature. Certainly, no likelier spot could be found for the survival of some great reptile from the Cretaceous or Jurassic eras, for there can be little doubt that the region's topography, vegetation and climate have scarcely changed at all over millions of years.

Perhaps only time will tell if the *mokele-mbembe* is something more than the imaginative perpetuation of a local myth, in both oral tradition and cave paintings. Whichever is the case, there are those modern investigators who believe the beast's fame spread far beyond the remote jungles of Central Africa. They suggest that the *mokele-mbembe* might very well be the *sirrush* or *mushhushshu*, a dragon-like beast depicted in bas-reliefs on the famous Ishtar Gate at Babylon and dating from about 600 BC. Disregarding the *sirrush*'s purely fabulous elements (the feet of both lion and eagle), they point, in particular, to its long tail, reptilian tongue, and above all to the curious, single horn projecting from its head – much as described by observers of its supposedly living counterpart. It is certainly true that the Ancient Babylonians knew something of the Congo River basin. There are also references to reptilian dragons in their mythology, as well as in the Biblical *Apocrypha*. Moreover, as we have seen elsewhere, it is possible to postulate certain existing reptile groups as the models for many of the dragons of a wide range of civilisations. Further than that, however, we can scarcely go.

MISSING LINKS

'Racialism' may have taken on something of a sinister connotation today, yet it is primarily only racial differences or origins that physically distinguish one group of men or women from another. Whether we are black, white, red, yellow, or some shade between, we are all one species (*Homo sapiens*), differing only in minor details, such as height, hair texture, and the accentuation or otherwise of facial features. The point is worth making, since it is unlikely that any other species of hominid exists on Earth today. If he does, he declines to compete with us and, indeed, if asked (and could respond) would probably only express a wish to be left in peace in those remote areas, perhaps high in the Himalayas or in the forests and swamps of North America, where rumour has it that he actually roams.

The question of whether such man-relatives, half-men, apemen, or whatever, really do exist concurrently with us has nevertheless exercised civilised man's imagination and intellect, and latterly his physical energies, for centuries. Their earliest manifestations were, of course, the semi-mythical giants discussed elsewhere, but apemen, too, crop up with some frequency in ancient and mediaeval lore, as well as in more recent descriptions. In 1613, an Englishman by the name of Andrew Battell told of encountering in the Congo region of Africa hairy man-like creatures that were of human likeness and height but twice as large in body and limbs. Other early accounts told of horrifying skirmishes with these *Untermenschen*, including the abduction and raping of women. Much later, more rational studies by zoologists like Dian Fossey and George Schaller demonstrated these great anthropoids' extreme inoffensiveness, although by this time their observations were less cause for wonder, since the subject of their studies was now known and recognised as man's nearest living evolutionary relative, the gorilla.

Thus legend becomes reality; yet the gorilla, for all its man-like attributes, is still only an ape, an animal. It is real half-men – men not quite like us but recognisably nearer to us in the evolutionary time-scale – that modern legend insists on keeping alive and has begun to emphasise, perhaps, ever since it became clear that there were gaps in our descending family tree. The most famous of these purported 'missing links' are the yeti or abominable snowman of Tibet and Nepal and the sasquatch or bigfoot of North America, but there are others which would appear to be more or less closely related, such as the Russian almas or wild men and the mudman or orang-dalam of Malaysia – the last-mentioned distinctive for its human-like modesty, in that it is said to wear a loincloth! Still more sub-men have been reported from the mountains of Central China and from Borneo, home of the original 'wild man', the orang-utan of zoology. While varying in certain details, with heights ranging from about 6 to 9 ft (2–3 m), all conform to a roughly similar physical pattern, with massive hairy bodies, almost neckless heads, on which there is commonly a pronounced sagittal crest, long arms reaching to the knees, and lurching, shambling gait. A recurrent theme is their repellent odour, reminiscent of rotting flesh, reported by those who claim to have been kidnapped by them. Smaller, pygmy versions are also alleged to exist, in the Himalayas, Indonesia, East Africa and the Colombian Andes, but they seem even less forthcoming than their giant brethren.

What, then, is the evidence for the existence of these intriguing creatures? To answer that one can only paraphrase the evasion so favoured by politicians and say it rather depends on what you mean by evidence. Certainly, no proven specimen, living or dead, has ever come under detailed scientific scrutiny, the nearest to it being the enigmatic Minnesota 'ice-man' which apparently deceived several experts when, preserved in a block of ice, it was exhibited at fairs in the United States in 1968. Rather significantly, the owner destroyed his ice-man when more concentrated interest began to be taken in it, and the consensus of opinion now seems to be that this supposed Neanderthal-relative was an elaborate fake. Similar explanations have been shown to lie behind other items of physical 'evidence', such as yeti scalps and mummified hands, the former made of serow goat-skin and the latter those of monkeys, probably the elusive Hanuman langur (*Presbytis entellus*), which exists in several races in the Himalayan and neighbouring mountain ranges, such as the Karkorams of Kashmir. Complete skins and hair samples, as well as droppings, have similarly turned out to be those of animals more or less familiar to western man. No modern skulls or bones, much less complete skeletons, have ever been found.

We are left with two other main kinds of so-called proof that apemen exist: actual sightings and discovery of their footprints and other signs of their presence. Both are numerous and indeed have shown such a steady increase in frequency of occurrence from about the middle of this century as to prompt the cynical suggestion that they have done so in direct proportion and response to popular interest in the creatures' existence. This would seem to be especially so in America, though to be fair one has to say that here, as elsewhere in the world, there is a more muted tradition of their presence among indigenous peoples. Indians from almost the whole length of North America's western coast, from Canada in the north as far south as Mexico, have a long tradition of belief in huge, man-like beings living in the mountains and forests which they refer to by different names, among them *sasquatch* or 'wild man of the woods'. Early white settlers apparently saw little of these elusive apemen, except their footprints, which were described as being of such huge size – twice the length and three times the width of a man's – that their creators became known as bigfoot: a name which has now come to be applied to all American phenomena of this type. From about the 1920s bigfoot itself began to be seen with increasing frequency and in all kinds of situations: sometimes apparently caught by surprise and glimpsed from a distance, on other occasions acting more openly. Reports tell of their being seen fishing from holes made in iced-over lakes, lifting huge boulders and (apparently) eating the rodents nesting beneath, and even occasionally waxing bold enough to peer into cars at startled drivers and passengers. Some even closer encounters dramatically reflect the Indians' traditional contention that bigfoot was in the habit of occasionally practising kidnapping. In 1924, for example, a Canadian lumberman camping in British Columbia told of being picked up in his sleeping-bag and carried by a bigfoot many miles away to its lair, where he was 'introduced' to the family – father, described as 8 ft (2.4 m) tall, the mother, a foot shorter, and two well grown children. It seems he managed to escape from their kindly but firm captivity but kept his strange experience to himself for thirty years, when he seems to have divulged it because other encounters with bigfoot were being made public and there was thus less risk of his being ridiculed. The linking of bigfoot with traditional lore is also reflected in other instances, as in the case of the woman who told of actually being raped by a bigfoot, thus updating those old myths of similarly rapacious gorillas.

For the most part, however, bigfoot seems content merely to let himself be seen. He is not, on the whole, aggressive, though by no means camera-shy. Most films and photographs of him are clearly fabrications, but one taken at Bluff Creek, Northern California, in 1967 has been regarded with more serious attention, both in America and Europe and in the USSR. This rather jumpy, hand-held sequence purports to show what would seem to be a female bigfoot, because of her pendulous breasts and protuberant buttocks, shambling in ape-like gait across a woodland clearing. I do not claim to be an authority but I have seen the film and can only say its 'star' looks most unconvincing, and many others share my view. Neither do the lady's footprints, subsequently found in the area, seem to tie in with what anthropologists have judged her height to be. Bigfoot seems, in fact, even more meticulous about leaving his (or her) footprints and trails for enthusiasts to puzzle over than he is about showing himself. Some such tracks comprise up to 3000 separate prints, with indications of the sort of extra weight on the ball of the foot, as well as length of stride, that one might expect of a creature leaving prints 17 in (43 cm) long and 7 in (18 cm) wide. If they are fakes, then the faker is a determined, clever and knowledgeable person.

An interesting and possibly significant point about America's famous apeman is that reports of him seem not only to be increasing in number but spreading in range, far inland from his traditional western home right across to the opposite coast, from Florida in the south northward to

Pennsylvania. Every state is determined to have its very own bigfoot, it seems.

Bigfoot's more famous Asian counterpart, the yeti of the Northern Himalayas of Nepal, Tibet, Bhutan and Sikkim, is considerably less forthcoming in every way and the evidence for his existence far more difficult to disentangle from local myth and folklore. Sightings by non-locals have been few and far between and usually tantalisingly distant, the inevitable implication being that they were really no more than some unidentified but known animal, such as langurs and bears, both of which are occasionally bipedal. Strange calls – screams, high-pitched howls and yelps or bird-like chirps – all tend to be associated with yetis by Nepalese Sherpas living at high altitude, but the utterers themselves seem wary of showing themselves, certainly to western eyes. Such footprints as have been found, and in some cases photographed, are far less humanoid or even ape-like than those of bigfoot and could easily be interpreted as having been made by known animals, more especially so since most trails are made in snow and, when exposed to sunshine, tend to spread and distort into shapes quite different from the original. One investigator actually proved the point by noting how 8-inch (20-cm) human footprints had, when he returned to the spot some 2–3 weeks later, become joined together and swollen to giant size, giving the impression of a monster bipedal track. Obviously, experienced investigators are aware of how misleading snow prints can be, and have gone to great lengths to make detailed comparative analyses of fresher and more intriguing trails, maintaining that they were unlikely to have been made by any known quadruped, ape or monkey; but the fact remains that they have not yet come up with any definite explanation as to what they *are*, unless of course we accept that yetis exist without more positive proof.

One of the great difficulties in the long-term pursuit of the abominable snowman lies in the somewhat mystical attitude of local Tibetans and Sherpas, who seem to waver between regarding the yeti as a living creature and as a semi-figurative bogey-man with which to cow their children into toeing the line, in a device that parents throughout the world have used since time immemorial. They also confuse matters for the western enquirer by insisting on applying the 'yeti' epithet both to a number of clearly identifiable animals, such as the langurs and bears mentioned earlier, and to less recognisable creatures, including man-beasts. They distinguish at least two kinds of human-like yeti, one large the other small. The first, called *dzu-teh* ('big creature') is a giant, some 8 ft (2.4 m) tall, and somewhat aggressively inclined, while the *meh-teh* ('man-like creature') is smaller and more mildly disposed. It is the former which they tell of killing yaks or even carrying off young girls, whereas the latter usually does little more than provide tantalising glimpses of

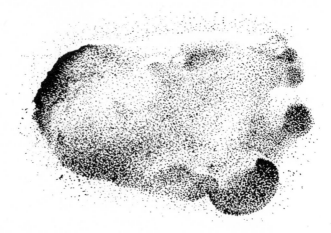

The most famous of yeti footprint photographs, from which this drawing was made, is that taken by Eric Shipton during his and Michael Ward's Everest Reconnaissance Expedition in 1951. One of a line of prints observed on the Menlung glacier, in Nepal, it measures 18 by 13 inches (45 by 33 cm) and 6½ inches (16.5 cm) across the heel. Most such prints can at least be tentatively identified or dismissed as doubtful but this one still puzzles experts and remains a mystery.

itself, including paying occasional visits to the gardens of mountain monasteries. Just how much of all this is calculated, myth-perpetuating story-telling or jokes at visitors' expense, or simply because the Tibetan and Sherpa attitude to life is so much less matter-of-fact and mystical than western man's, is anyone's guess.

Not to be outdone, both the Russians and the Chinese tell of their own wild men, in many different parts of a vast area ranging from the Caucasus Mountains, eastward to the Pamirs of Soviet Turkestan, the Gobi Desert and Central China, and north to Siberia. Rumours of apemen in Mongolia date back to the 1880s when Przewalski, discoverer of the wild horse that now bears his name, heard folk tales to this effect, but there are numerous later accounts of actual encounters, including invasion of camps and the stoning of a village by apemen during exceptionally severe weather. Some Russian 'almas' have been reported as shot but for one reason or another no bodies have ever been recovered (at least, so far as we in the west know). In China, several reports of sub-men emanate from the mountains of Central Hunan province, and in early 1985 some popular excitement was caused by news that a diminutive apeman or child, about 3 ft 6 in (1 m) tall, had actually been captured.

Unfortunately for crypto-zoologists it proved to be a rare short-tailed monkey.

Those who take the subject seriously, and refuse to believe that the myriad tales of apeman sightings can be explained in terms acceptable to sceptical zoologists, offer a number of theories to account for them. Among the more moderate is the possibility of the survival of the orang-utan in Central Asia, where fossils indicate that the ape did once exist, though it is now known only from Borneo and Sumatra. More extravagantly, others have suggested that Asiatic apemen might be the last survivors of *Gigantopithecus*, a gorilla-like ape, whose remains have been discovered in India and China, or, rather closer to modern man, a latter-day *Homo neanderthalensis*. The American bigfoot presents difficulties in the way of both explanations, of course, although it is just possible that both *Gigantopithecus* and Neanderthal man could have found their way to North America from Asia via the then-existing land-bridge now separated by the Bering Strait. If nothing else, it may be that early tales of huge sub-men came to the American Indians by this route, thus contributing to a groundwork of folklore.

All, however, is conjecture, and the only certain thing is that the yeti and bigfoot, in particular, have now become both scientifically acceptable subjects of research and big business. Both the Russians and the Chinese now have special scientific departments devoted to their study and the organisation of expeditions in search of them. International conferences are held, during which serious scientific papers are read on apemen. In America, certain states now take bigfoot so seriously that they have decreed he must not be shot, and a whole tourist industry has been built up around him, even to the extent of a statue in Willow Creek, California, and a periodical devoted entirely to his doings. The governments of Nepal, Tibet and Bhutan now openly advertise themselves as 'the lands of the yeti'.

It would be idle to speculate further on whether 'half-men' exist or not, certainly not without greater evidence. Given all the data available, the likeliest explanations of this semi-scientific phenomenon still seem to lie in myth, mistaken identity, self-delusion or deliberate faking. If the last, it would certainly be no novelty, for the creation of animal frauds has a long history and even reputable scientists are not above perpetrating what might be called 'in' jokes. One in this particular context was, of course, the famous Piltdown Man, 'discovered' in 1912 and accepted as a valid, if puzzling, fossil hominid for forty years, until detailed analysis showed it to be a combination of relatively modern human skull and the jaw of an orang-utan. But at least Piltdown Man's milieu was right, for if 'missing links' are to be discovered it is far more likely that they will be found in fossil strata than as living, breathing apemen.

BIBLIOGRAPHY

Armstrong, E.A. (1958), *The Folklore of Birds*, Collins, London.

Beaty, J.Y. (1943), *Nature is stranger than fiction*, Harrap, London.
Breland, O.P. (1950), *Animal Facts and Fallacies*, Faber, London.
Brown, J.A.C. (1977), *Pears Medical Encyclopedia*, Pelham, London.
Burton, M. (1955), *Animal Legends*, Muller, London.
Burton, M. (1978), *Just Like an Animal*, Dent, London.
Burton, M. (1979), *A Zoo at Home*, Dent, London.
Burton, R. (1980), *The Life and Death of Whales*, Deutsch, London.

Camp, J. (1973), *Magic, Myth and Medicine*, Priory Press/Wayland, Hove.
Canning, J. (1971), *50 Great Horror Stories*, Souvenir Press, London.
Caras, R. (1976), *Dangerous to Man: the Definitive Story of Wildlife's Reputed Dangers*, Barrie & Jenkins, London.
Carrington, R. (1957), *Mermaids and Mastodons*, Chatto & Windus, London.
Clair, C. (1967), *Unnatural History: An Illustrated Bestiary*, Abelard-Schumann, London.
Copley, G.J. (1963), *Names and Places*, Dent, London.

Dance, P. (1976), *Animal Fakes and Frauds*, Sampson Low, Maidenhead.
Dinsdale, T. (1972), *Loch Ness Monster*, Routledge & Kegan Paul, London.

Evans, B. (1947), *The Natural History of Nonsense*, Michael Joseph, London.

George, J. & others (1964), *Marvels & Mysteries of Our Animal World*, Reader's Digest Assoc., New York.
Gibson, F. (1905), *Superstitions about Animals*, Walter Scott.
Gould, C. (1886), *Mythical Monsters*, W.H. Allen, London.
Grigson, G. (1962), *The Shell Country Book*, Phoenix House, London.

Guirand, P. (Ed.) (1962), *The Larousse Encyclopedia of Mythology*, Hamlyn, Feltham, Middlesex.

Halstead, B.W. (1978), *Poisonous and Venomous Marine Animals of the World*, Darwin Press, Princeton, New Jersey.

Heuvelmans, B. (1962), *On the Track of Unknown Animals*, Hart-Davis, London.

Hart, M. (1982), *Rats*, Allison & Busby, London and New York.

Hulme, F.E. (1985), *Natural History Lore and Legend*, Quaritch, London.

Humburg, N. (1984), *Der Rattenfänger von Hameln*, Verlag C.W. Niemeyer, Hameln.

Hutchins, J. (1968), *Discovering Mermaids and Sea Monsters*, Shire, Princes Risborough, Bucks.

Hyams, E. (1972), *Animals in the Service of Man: 10,000 Years of Domestication*, Dent, London.

Inwards, R. (1950), *Weather Lore*, Rider & Co., London and New York/S.R. Publishers, East Ardsley, Wakefield (1969 reprint).

Jackson, C.E. (1968), *British Names of Birds*, Witherby, London.

Krappe, A.H. (1930), *The Science of Folklore*, Methuen, London.

Landsburg, A. (1977), *In Search of Myths and Monsters*, Transworld Publishers, London.

Lane, F.W. (1957), *Kingdom of the Octopus*, Jarrold, Norwich.

Lehner, E. & J. (1969), *A Fantastic Bestiary: Beasts and Monsters in Myth and Folklore*, Tudor Publishing Co., New York.

Ley, W. (1952), *The Lungfish, the Dodo and the Unicorn*, Viking Press, New York.

Lindsay, B. (1973), *Monsters of the Sea*, Scholastic Book Services, London and New York, etc.

Lopez, B.H. (1978), *Of Wolves and Men*, Dent, London.

Mackal, R.P. (1983), *Searching for Hidden Animals: An Inquiry into Zoological Mysteries*, Cadogan Books, London.

Mackenzie, D.A. (n.d.), *Teutonic Myth and Legend; Egyptian Myth and Legend; Indian Myth and Legend; Myths of Babylonia and Assyria; Myths of Crete and Pre-Hellenic Europe; Myths of China and Japan; Myths of Pre-Columbian America*, Gresham Publishing Co., London.

Mansell, F. (1940), *The Wayfarer's Book*, Ward Lock, London.

Maple, E. (1971), *Superstition and the Superstitious*, W.H. Allen, London.

Marriott, P.J. (1981), *Red Sky at Night: Weather Lore of the English Countryside: 1900 sayings explained and tested*, Sheba Books, Oxford.

McEwan, G.J. (1978), *Sea Serpents, Sailors and Sceptics*, Routledge & Kegan Paul, London.

Melville, J. (1977), *Phobias and Obsessions*, Allen & Unwin, London.

Moncrieff, A.R.H. (n.d.), *Classic Myth and Legend; Romance and Legend of Chivalry*, Gresham Publishing Co., London.

Morris, D. (1979), *Animal Days*, Cape, London.

Napier, J. (1972), *Bigfoot: The Yeti and Sasquatch in Myth and Reality*, Cape, London.

Newall, V. (1977), *Discovering the Folklore of Birds and Beasts*, Shire, Princes Risborough, Bucks.

Oudermans, A.C. (1892), *The Great Sea Serpent*, E.J. Brill, Leiden; Luzac, London.

Pereira, J. (1840), *The Elements of Materia Medica*, Part II, Longman, Orme, Brown, Green, and Longmans, London.

Potter, S. and Sargeant, L. (1973), *Pedigree: Words from Nature*, Collins, London.

Robinson, H.S. and Wilson, K. (1962), *The Encyclopaedia of Myths and Legends of All Nations*, Kaye & Ward, London.

Schul, B. (1978), *The Psychic Power of Animals*, Coronet Books/Hodder & Stoughton, Sevenoaks.

Simmonds, P.J. (1885), *The Animal Food Resources of Different Nations*, E. & F.N. Spon, London and New York.

Squire, C. (n.d.), *Celtic Myth and Legend, Poetry and Romance*, Gresham Publishing Co. London.

Stenuit, R. (1968), *The Dolphin, Cousin to Man*, Dent, London.

Taberner, P. (1985), *Aphrodisiacs: The Science and the Myth*, Croom Helm, London.

Thompson, C.J.S. (1930), *The Mystery and Lore of Monsters*, Williams & Norgate, London.

Watson, L. (1973), *Supernature: A Natural History of the Supernatural*, Hodder & Stoughton, London.

Welfare, S. and Fairley, J. (1980), *Arthur C. Clarke's Mysterious World*, Collins, London.

INDEX

Page numbers in *italics* refer to illustrations.

Aesop, 59
Alice in Wonderland, 16
Amphibians, 21, 43, 45–47, *46,* 50, *62–63,* 92, 93, 110, 112, 140–141
Androcles, 69
Anglo-Saxons, 14, 26, 27, 88
Animal Gods, 14, 28–33, 40, 43, 58, 59, 103, *113,* 120, 127, 128, 133, 138–139
Animals, Mythical, 7, 8, 27–30, *29,* 40, 47, 48, 75, 77, 88, 91, 100, 126–142, 149, 151
Antelopes, 84, 130, 131, 143
Arabia/Arabs, 48, 98, 106, 109, 126–128, 130, 139
Arabian Nights, The, 126
Aristotle, 141
Atlantic, 86, 91, 144
Attila the Hun, 67
Aztecs of Mexico, 112, 138

Babylonians and Assyrians, 119, 139, 149
Badgers, 12, 27, 35, 59, *60,* 93, 101
Bats, 10, 12, 75–77, *74, 77,* 132, 143
Battell, Andrew, 150
Batten, H. Mortimer, 52
Bears, 11, 13, 14, 17, 44, 89, 101, 102, 112, 113, 119, 130, 153
Beast-men, 7, 14, 27–30, 88, 119, 136–139, 149–155, *154*
Bible, The Holy, 11, 14, 17, 20, 30, 31, 70, 89, 132, 137, 140, 149
Birds, 7, 9–15, 17, 20, 23–32, *32,* 34–37, 57, 60–64, 67, 68, 79, 90–92, 94, 102, 111, 112, 114, 116, 121–124, *122–129,* 132, 134, 136, 143, 149

Blackmore, R. D., 101
Bosch, Hieronymus, 78
Browning, Robert, 115, 118-119
Buckland, William, 47
Burroughs, Edgar Rice, 119
Burton, Maurice, 123, 128

Cannibalism, 10, 41–43, 49–50, 73, 138
Caras, Robert, 72
Cats, Big, 11, 29–31, 44, 69, 82, 89, 101, 119, 121, 132
Cats, Domestic, 14, 25, 27, 28, 34–36, 48, 60, 63, 68, 89, 91, 92, 103–104, *113,* 114, 134, 139
Cattle and Oxen, 7, 12, 13, 17, 26, 27, 34, 35, 77, 82, 84, 101, 102, 112, 123, 124, 155
Celts, 136
Centipedes and Millipedes, 18, 85
Cetaceans (whales, dolphins, porpoises), 17, 57–59, 62, 69, 89, 90, 103, *129,* 130, 134, 135, 146, 148
Charlemagne, 59
Cicero, 59
Civet 'cat', 102–103
Cleopatra, 40, 132, 140
Coelenterates (jellyfish etc.), 17, 77, 98, 140, 141
Columba, St 144–145
Columbus, Christopher, 139
Cook, Captain James, 112
Crete, Ancient, 102, 119
Crocodilians, 16, 31, 41, 43, 94, 112, 127, 133, 141
Crustaceans, 16–19, *18,* 52, 94, 98, 111, 145

Deer, 28, 77, 84, 100, 102, 130
Dioscorides, 103, 105

Dogs, 9, 13, 15, 26, 34–36, 45, 58, 60, 63, 68, 71, 88, 89, 89, 92, 100, 102, 113–114, 116, 119–121, 146, 148
Dolbear, A. E., 65
Doyle, Sir Arthur Conan, 98, 144

Edemtates (sloth, armadillo), 11, 12, 112
Egyptians, Ancient, *29,* 31–33, *33,* 40, 43, 102, *113,* 114, 119, 127, 128, 140
Eikai, Satake, 55
Elephants, 14, 15, 31, 37, 38, 89, 100, 126, 130, 145
Etruscans, 121

Fishes, 16, 18–21, *21,* 28, 30, 31, 41, 51, 53, 59, 62, 63, 65–67, 89, 94–96, 100, 111, 112, 134, 143, 146–148
Fossey, Dian, 150
Foxes, 12, 35, 44, 45, 61, 93

Galen, 104
Gennaro, J. F., 131
Giants, 7, 27, 47, 48, 136–138, 150–155
Goats, 14, 30, 112, 119, 138, 151
Gray, Thomas, 22
Greek, Ancient, 28–32, *32,* 58, 59, 69, 91, 102, 103, 105, 109, 112, 127–130, 132, 136–142
Grimm, Jacob and Wilhelm, 115
Grimond, Jo, 60

Hannibal, 37
Hedgehog, 20, 43, 44, 101, 123–125, *124*
Herodotus, 59, 127, 128
Hippocrates, 105

159

Hittites, *29,* 30
Holland, Philemon, 25
Horses and other equines, 7, 12, 22, 27, 37, 58, 64, 68, 82, 85, 101, 102, 129, 130, 134, 138, 143, 145, 148, 154
Hosking, Eric, 91
Howell, James, 118

Incas of Peru, 138
Insects, 9–13, 16, 18, 19, 21–25, *24,* 27, 28, 30, 32, *33,* 36, 41, 45–51, 56–58, 61, 62, 64, 65, 75–77, 79–87, *83, 87,* 93, 104–108, *106, 107,* 113, 117, 125, 128, 129
Ivan IV, 'The Terrible', 195

John the Evangelist, St, 31
Johnston, Sir Harry, 143

Kidd, Captain, 98
Kipling, Rudyard, 40, 43, 120

Lake monsters, 7, 135, 144–149, *147*
Language, animals in the, 7, 9–37, 40, 41, 44, 46, 51, 69, 80, 84–87, 96, 109, 122, 132, 133, 138
Leeches, 18, 66–67, 66, 85, 109–110
Levin, Bernard, 78
Lizards, 19, 20, 35, 36, 80, 93, 94, 133, 140, 141
Llama, 31

Mackal, Roy, 135, 148
Mammals, 9–17, 20, 22, 26–31, 34–38, 43–45, 47, 48, 52–64, 67–77, 79, 82, 84, 88–94, 99–102, 110, 112–121, 123–126, *129,* 130, 132, 134–139, 142, 143, 145, 146, 148–155
Man, Prehistoric, 100, 150, 151, 155
Mandeville, Sir John, 48
Mark, St, 30, 62
Marsupials (kangaroo, opossum etc.), 15, 17, 31, 89
Martial, 43
Medicine, Animals in, 8, *18,* 31, 85–87, 99–114, *129,* 130
Mediterranean, 20, 28, 106, 132, 140

Merryweather, Dr, 67
Michael, St, 132
Mills, 'Brusher', 41
Molluscs, 17, 18, 23, 28, 94, 96–98, 110, 111, 131, 135, 140
Mongooses, 43, 44, 56
Morris, Desmond, 70
Mowat, Farley, 89

Norsemen, 58, 104, 130, 131, 133

Octopus, 94, 96, 97, 131, 135, 140
Otters, 27, 61, 134, 146

Pacific, 59, 79, 97, 112, 131, 132, 139, 143, 148
Peter, St, 20
Phoenicians, 28
Pigs, 12, 14, 20, 26, 119
Place-names, Animal, 24–27, 133
Platypus, Duck-billed, 90, 143
Pliny the Elder, 22, 25, 59, 112, 132, 141
Plutarch, 59, 67
Poe, Edgar Allan, 73
Polar regions, 90, 134, 135
Pollaiuolo, Antonio, 121
Polynesians, 59, 112
Ponoppidan, Bishop Erik, 131
Primates (apes, monkeys etc.), 16, 17, 29, 70, 72, 89, 119, 138, 150–155
Przewalski, Nikolai, 154
Pygmies, 27, 138, 148, 151
Pyrrhus, 37

Rabbits and hares, 12, 41, 101
Raccoons, 15
Reptiles, 7, 9, 13, 16, 17, 20, 21, 31, 32, 35, 36, 38–44, *39, 42.* 47, 70–72, 79, 83, 84, 93, 94, *103,* 104, 112, 127, 129, 132, 133, 134, 136, 140–145, 147, 149
Rhinoceros, 89, 100, 101, 130
Rines, Robert, 145
Robinson, E. Kay, 76, 136
Rodents, 11–13, 15, 17, 22, 26, 37, 41, 44, 52–57, *55,* 59, 62, 72–75, 102, 103, 114–119, 152
Romans, Ancient, 14, 22, 25, 28–31, 37, 40, 43, 58, 59, 67, 82, 104, 105, 109, 119, 121, 130, 132, 139, 141, 142
Romulus and Remus, 119, 121
Ryabchikov, Prof. A. M., 146

Schaller, George, 150
Schul, Bill, 69
Scott, Sir Peter, 144
Sea-anemones, 141
Sea-serpents and sea-monsters, 27, 41, 130–136
Seals, 90, 134, 135, 139, 146
Shakespeare, 13–15, 92, 138
Sheep, 12, 14, 27, 45, 63, 101, 102, 112, 135, 145
Shiels, Anthony, 145
Shipton, Eric, 154
Shipton, Mother, 22
Shrews, 13, 90, 91, 102
Singh, Rev. J. A. L., 120, 121
Sirenians (dugong, manatee), 29, 139
Slugs and snails, 23, 110, 111
Snakes, 9, 13, 21, 31, 32, 35, 38–44, *39, 42,* 70–72, 79, 83, 84, 93, 94, *103,* 104, 112, 114, 132–134, 136, 140, 141
Spiders, Scorpions and other Arachnids, 9, 10, 16, 18, 47–50, 57, 61, 78–80, 84, 85, 107, *108,* 126, 129, 143
Sponges, Freshwater, 111
Squid, 94, 96, 97, 131, 135, 140
Starfish, 17
Symbols, Animal, 11, 26, 30–33, *32, 33,* 40, 41, *103,* 111, 127, 128, 130

Teutons, 136
Topsell, Rev. E., 100, 112, 130
Tortoises and Turtles, 17, 94
Tunicates, 135, 136
Turkey, 109, 117

Valentine, St, 62
Valentine and Orson, 119
Verne, Jules, 97
Virgil, 82
Virgin Mary, 20, 22
Vitus, St, 118

Ward Michael, 154
Wardlow, Robert Pershing, 137
Weasels, stoats etc., 5, 8, 10–12, 20, 26, 53, 59, *90*
Weather, Animals and the, 8, 20, 62–67, 88
Wells, H. G., 37,
White, Gilbert, 102
Wilson, Dr. R. K., 145
Wolsey, Cardinal, 78
Wolves, 26, 88, 89, 119–121
Worms, 9, 11, 19, 46, 50, 51, 65, 66, 85, 109, 110